Criminal Tax Secrets: What Every Defense Attorney Should Know

An Insider's Guide to Evaluating Every Stage of a Criminal Tax Investigation

Robert Nordlander

Nordlander CPA, PLLC

Nordlander CPA, PLLC

First edition

Paperback ISBN: 979-8-9871373-0-7

Kindle ISBN: 979-8-9871373-1-4

To my family:
Thank you for your patience in writing this book.

***

To the IRS-CI coworkers, federal prosecutors, and probation officers:
Thank you for your hard work and sharing your wisdom during my career.

***

To my forensic accounting and fraud examiner friends:
Thank you for the inspiration to publish.

Contents

Disclaimer

E very effort has been made for the content of this book to be accurate. Be aware that I am not an attorney. I am not licensed to practice law or give legal advice. Any advice I give in this book is based on my over 20-year experience as a special agent with IRS Criminal Investigation (IRS-CI). If you asked me privately how I would approach a criminal tax investigation, the content of this book is what I would consider in evaluating your case.

The purpose of this book is to share my thoughts and my experience. I spent over two decades in the field investigating tax fraud, advising federal prosecutors, developing training for special agents, supervising other special agents, and mentoring new agents as they started their careers.

For every rule in criminal law, tax law, policy, or procedure, there are multiple exceptions to the rule. The assumption is that you have a basic understanding of representing a defendant in federal court. The purpose of this book is to pull back the curtain on how decisions are made in a criminal tax investigation from an IRS-CI special agent's perspective. Federal prosecutors present the case in court, but special agents evaluate, investigate, advise, and recommend charges. As much as I respect the responsibility of attorneys, the investigation rises and falls on the investigator and the quality of their work. A firm understanding of their work product and obstacles gives you discernment on what a reasonable outcome should be for your client. My goal is to give you insightful information so that you can better advise your client how to resolve their criminal tax problems.

So, please read the book, enjoy the information, and consider the options that I recommend, but this book is not a legal treatise; it is not meant to cover all possibilities and outcomes. However, as an experienced adviser to criminal tax attorneys, this is how I evaluate their cases.

Why this Book?

This book is for attorneys who practice criminal tax defense in federal court. After many months or years investigating a federal tax crime, the culmination of my efforts as a special agent was to recommend tax violation charges and who should be a defendant versus a witness. Federal court is where my investigation efforts were tested by the prosecutor, defense counsel, jury, and judge. To get an investigation ready for trial, the evidence had to be convincing enough for a jury to convict and a judge to sentence active prison time. That was the standard by which IRS-CI operated: straight forward, no bluffing, solid cases.

This book can be beneficial to other professionals, but its purpose is specifically for defense attorneys who already understand the procedures, law, and rules applicable in federal court.

Criminal tax violations represent a small percentage of all criminal cases in federal court. As a criminal defense attorney, you know that criminal tax is a specialty and requires a different skill set. It is a slightly different animal than white collar defense and definitely different than the gun and drug violations that most defense attorneys see on a daily basis.

As an IRS-CI special agent, I conducted many criminal tax and money laundering investigations throughout my career. The cases ranged from simple embezzlement that resulted in unreported income to tax evasion using foreign trusts. Some cases were topics on daytime TV, national news, PBS, The New

York Times, and various magazines. Throughout all this, I met with many defense attorneys. Some were stellar and worth every penny; others caused their clients more problems than if the defendants represented themselves. The good ones asked questions and pushed back when necessary. The bad ones made outlandish statements without evidence, stalled, and left their client with little negotiation room with the prosecutors.

An attorney friend compared working with good attorneys to playing billiards. He was right. When someone just likes to smack the balls around, no one learns anything. Playing with professionals, however, can be deeply instructive. I have worked with and against many professionals, and have learned a great deal about what goes into the perfect shot.

Whether meeting with a federal prosecutor, defense attorney, or the US probation officer as a federal criminal investigator, I was the resource that explained the charges, tax loss, and potential enhancements at sentencing. Many times, I was sharing the same wisdom. In all my meetings with criminal defense attorneys, I never saw a financial and tax expert in criminal tax violations on their team. Being the sole financial and tax expert in the room during meetings put the defense at a disadvantage. The defense attorneys had to rely on my expertise in evaluating their clients willfulness, potential tax loss, and negate the possible reliance defense. Being trustworthy is critical as a criminal investigator, but we can make mistakes. This book is to help you determine if mistakes were made by the government.

Throughout the course of a criminal tax investigation, these questions were part of my evaluation process:

- Should this case be open or closed?

- What are the weaknesses and strengths of the investigation?

- Who should be a witness or a defendant?

- Does this investigation meet the mission of IRS-CI?

- Is there a better way to prosecute this case?

This book sums up best practices in evaluating criminal tax cases. My mission is to help defense attorneys in federal court better understand the inner workings of a criminal tax investigation, make the good attorneys better, and help defense attorneys who take criminal tax cases be comfortable in analyzing their clients' options.

I am going to pull back the curtain so you know how decisions are made, how you can evaluate your clients' options (pre- and post- indictment), and how you can get the best outcome possible for your clients — whether a complete dismissal of charges, a reasonable plea bargain, or a fair hearing at sentencing. At the end of this book, you will be able to fully evaluate all the evidence against your client and in your client's favor. With that knowledge, you can get the best outcome possible. This book can't change the facts in an investigation or the lie of the balls on the billiard table, but it will help you take the best shot for your client.

Here on out, I am going to walk you through the process:

- How a civil audit becomes a criminal tax investigation and how you can keep it out of criminal court.

- How IRS-CI evaluates its cases for criminal investigation.

- How to evaluate your options pre-indictment. (Yes, the IRS can be persuaded to close a case).

- How to decipher possible weaknesses in various tax charges.

- What should be in discovery (that probably isn't).

- How to give your clients their best chance at trial and sentencing.

Keep reading. You are about to change your perspective on criminal tax cases. Instead of relying on the government's case agent (as most criminal defense attorneys do in this situation), you will understand the strengths and weaknesses of the typical criminal tax investigation. You will know exactly what to review, what questions to ask, and what documents to analyze.

Chapter 1

The Role of Criminal Tax Investigations

L ike all government agencies, the IRS has a mission statement:

> "To provide American taxpayers top quality service by helping
> them understand and meet their tax responsibilities and by ap-
> plying the tax law with integrity and fairness to all."

The general public might disagree with the "top quality service," but this
mission to have all citizens meet their tax obligations is accurate. Compliance
in properly reporting and paying taxes is the top priority for the IRS.

IRS-CI has a slightly different but similar mission:

> "To serve the American public by investigating potential crimi-
> nal violations of the internal revenue code, and related financial
> crimes in a manner that fosters confidence in the tax system in
> compliance with the tax law."

Fostering confidence in the tax system means that the general public knows about successful criminal tax investigations. Once the general public sees an article, video, or reads a press release reporting a defendant receiving active prison time and fines, the public has confidence that if their next-door neighbor who owns a business is cheating on their taxes, he is going to get caught. Therefore, everybody is playing by the same set of rules in compliance with the law.

Ultimately, IRS-CI's goal is to stop people from misbehaving. In some cases, the resources of IRS-CI are used as the last stop in a long effort to get the taxpayer to behave. Sometimes, the taxpayer has misbehaved through earning illegal income, and IRS-CI is used as the hammer to put a stop to the criminal activity. However, IRS-CI's bread-and-butter investigations are legal income cases, which only IRS-CI can investigate.

Most crimes are greed related. A bookkeeper creates false companies to steal money from her employer. A con artist persuades an elderly person to invest money in a scheme. A drug dealer robs another drug dealer, or there is a turf war between two rival factions. Their crimes are not because of passion, but of greed. Crimes of greed typically fall within the jurisdiction of IRS-CI's tax and money laundering expertise.

When a defense attorney understands the mission of IRS-CI, it creates options for getting the best deal possible. A laser like focus can be accomplished by knowing what IRS-CI is looking for and why..

As it stands in 2021, IRS-CI has slightly over 2,000 special agents nationwide.[1] It is a small part of the whole tax assessment and collection business.

With that in mind, let's look into when a civil function such as an audit or collection activity uncovers a taxpayer's actions that are perceived to be a tax crime. When that time comes, IRS-CI is vital because it is considered the government's last option to get a taxpayer into compliance.

With IRS having a dual function of civil and criminal tax investigations, there are instances when the civil function believes that a crime has been committed. That is the topic of the next chapter.

---

1. 2021 IRS Crim. Investigation Ann. Rep. 3

Chapter 2

When a Civil Audit Becomes a Criminal Tax Investigation

At times, the IRS civil section discovers suspicious activity during its routine business of audits and collections that gives rise to a belief that a tax crime was committed. As part of their duties, they are supposed to be watching for tax crimes to refer to IRS-CI.

It's rare for such a referral to be the source of a criminal investigation, but it does happen. The IRS civil section, however, is the favorite source of tax investigations for IRS-CI. According to the 2021 IRS-CI Annual Report, approximately 7% of all investigations conducted by IRS-CI were directly a result of a civil fraud referral becoming a criminal tax investigation Both IRS and IRS-CI want more fraud referrals coming from audits and collections.[1] IRS

---

1. 2021 IRS Crim. Investigation Ann. Rep. 3

created the Office of Fraud Enforcement in 2020, which is focused on finding and referring potential tax crimes to IRS-CI.[2]

This chapter is not about voluntary disclosure, particularly taxpayers with undisclosed foreign bank accounts. This chapter is also not about when an IRS-CI special agent finds a case on his own initiative. IRS-CI special agents do look for their own cases and are evaluated on their ability to find quality tax crimes to investigate. There are some parts in these chapters that will overlap when there is an actual criminal investigation outside of a fraud referral from the civil side.

This chapter is about a civil examination potentially becoming a criminal tax investigation. In IRS lingo, this is called a "fraud referral."

You may find yourself in a situation where the IRS hasn't opened a criminal tax investigation, but the facts create the potential to open one. A civil attorney may have concerns about their client's tax problems and talk to you about it. This chapter will assist you in evaluating the facts that are concerning to that civil attorney. Based on this knowledge, you can then advise them on the next step.

Main Function of Civil Side of IRS

Most of IRS's business is a civil function consisting of two major areas: the assessment of tax and the collection of tax. An assessment of tax starts when a tax return is filed. When a tax return is filed, the taxpayer self-assesses their tax liability: they tell the government what they believe is their tax bill. The taxpayer reports how much is owed and how much has been paid; the difference is either a tax liability or a refund. Since it is self-assessed, there is no IRS employee involved in the process.

---

2. James Lee & Damon Rowe, IRS Priorities: Detecting Fraud, Protecting Taxpayers (Nov. 19, 2021), Internal Revenue Service, https://www.irs.gov/about-irs/irs-priorities-detecting-fraud-protecting-taxpayers.

Matching Information to Tax Returns

Most of the letters that taxpayers receive in the mail are from matching the tax return with third party records that were sent to the IRS. The most common example is when the taxpayer sells stock held in a brokerage account but he forgets to put the sale on the tax return. The IRS compares the tax return with the information it received from the brokerage company. That difference is referenced in a notice mailed to the taxpayer, and an additional tax is assessed, which also includes penalty and interest. This is not an audit, but is most commonly referred to as an audit by a taxpayer.

Audits

Audits are typically generated in an area that the IRS wants to focus its tax enforcement; it could be a particular industry or line items on the tax return. The exact criteria is held in secret and could change over time. To ensure compliance in a particular industry, the IRS will focus its efforts on auditing companies in that industry.

According to the IRS 2020 Data Book, the overall chance of being audited is less than 1%. For a taxpayer with over $500,000 in income, the audit rates increased to between 1.1% to 8.6%, depending on the income level.[3]

Unfiled Tax Returns

Along the same line of thought as the matching of tax return information with third party information is the catching of non-filers. If a taxpayer hasn't filed a tax return, but a third-party reports their income, the IRS will send a letter to the taxpayer, asking for a tax return. If a taxpayer does not file a tax return, the

---

3. IRS Statement: Updated IRS Audit Numbers (May 26, 2022), Internal Revenue Service, https://www.irs.gov/pub/irs-utl/statement-for-update d-audit-rates-ty-19.pdf

IRS will create a "substitute for return" (SFR). Per section 6020(b) of U.S.C. Title 26, the IRS is authorized to create a tax return and assess a tax on behalf of the taxpayer using reasonable information.[4] In IRS lingo this is called "6020B." Those are the main methods that the IRS uses to assess taxes. The taxpayer can file a tax return, a mistake can be caught, an audit can ensue, or the IRS can prepare the tax return for the taxpayer.

Collections

Another side of civil tax enforcement is collections. Collections activity starts when a tax is owed. To collect those taxes, the IRS has employees (called revenue officers) who go out into the field to meet taxpayers, assess the taxpayer's ability to pay, and make decisions on how the taxes will be collected.

Many times during an economic downturn, payroll taxes are withheld from employee paychecks but are not deposited into the United States Treasury. The withheld taxes are not paid because it's an easy piggy bank to borrow from in order to pay bills and to keep the business afloat. In due time, revenue officers will notify the business that payroll taxes are owed. The taxpayer will be asked how and when the IRS can expect to receive payment.

Though payroll taxes can be substantial, revenue officers are also tasked with collecting other types of taxes, including income taxes and excise taxes. If a taxpayer is not paying what they're required, the IRS revenue officer can levy assets and income, file liens, and pursue the sale of assets.

Where Fraud Referrals Frequently Occur

Between audits and collections, the IRS's collection function is the greatest generator of leads for fraud referrals to IRS-CI. When payment is required and the IRS is getting aggressive to collect, taxpayers start scheming to hide

---

4. I.R.C. § 6020(b) (2022)

assets and income. When there is a fraud referral, almost always it's from the revenue officer trying to collect back taxes; it is rarely from the assessment side of IRS. Fraud referrals don't originate from mistakes that were found in matching returns to third party records. Nor are fraud referrals coming solely from unfiled tax returns. In my experience, I have never seen a fraud referral from the assessment function; it has always been from the collection side. The tax has already been assessed, and the revenue officer is at their wit's end trying to collect from someone who appears to have the ability to pay but keeps moving money around or has a lifestyle that is inconsistent with what is being reported.

Typically, the revenue officer will notify the taxpayer of the tax liability, and will request records of assets and income to determine how the taxpayer can pay, where to levy wages and record liens, etc. This happens after the IRS has sent notices for many months in the mail to the taxpayer about the past due taxes. If there are any missing tax returns, the revenue officer will demand those too, because it streamlines the collection process. The IRS doesn't know the true tax amount owed or what tax is owed (payroll, excise, or income) if the tax return is not filed. The missing tax returns give a picture of the remaining taxes owed.

It is during this time that the revenue officer either will not receive information from the taxpayer, will receive false documents, or the taxpayer will lie to the revenue officer about their assets and income. Some sophisticated schemes include placing income and assets in a nominee name or alter ego. The range of fraud runs the gamut from as simple as misusing the corporate credit card to pay for personal living expenses to placing assets and income overseas.

When collection officers become aggressive, the taxpayer will contact an attorney or CPA to help pull the IRS off their back. It is a long process from when the taxpayer is on the IRS's radar screen to assigning a revenue officer to collect the missing tax returns and balance due. But once the collection process starts, the taxpayer can expect more adverse collection practices until the taxpayer starts to comply.

The rest of this chapter is to help you understand the procedural and evaluation process that takes place when the civil function starts to become a criminal investigation.

Badges of Fraud

Revenue agents (auditors) and revenue officers (collections) are trained to look for badges of fraud during an examination. Badges of fraud are described in Internal Revenue Manual (IRM) section 25.1.2.3.[5]

In theory, their eyes are to be open to the following characteristics of fraud as shown in IRM section 25.1.2.3. Here are some examples:

- Omitting entire sources of income.

- Failing to report or explain substantial amounts of income identified as received.

- Substantial personal expenditures exceeding reported income.

- Failing to file tax returns for several years.

- Cashing checks at check cashing services and at banks.

- Making false description of receipts.

- Claiming fictitious or substantially overstated deductions.

- Claiming personal living expenses as business expenses.

- Multiple sets of books.

- False entries or documents.

- Checks made payable to third parties that are endorsed back to the taxpayer.

---

5. Internal Revenue Service, U.S. Dep't of Treasury, Internal Revenue Manual § 25.1.2.3 (2021), available at https://www.irs.gov/irm/part25/irm_25-001-002

- Attempt to hinder or obstruct the examination by failing to answer questions and refusing to provide records.

- Failure to make full disclosure of relevant facts to the accountant, attorney or return preparer.

- Destruction of books and records, especially if just after examination was started.

- Transfer of assets for purposes of concealment.

- Asset ownership placed in other names.

- Transfer made in anticipation of a tax assessment or while the investigation of a deficiency is pending.

- Use of secret bank accounts for income.

- Deposits into bank accounts under nominee names.

- Conduct of business transactions in false names.

Badges of fraud can ultimately become a criminal prosecution. As mentioned before, approximately 7% of the open criminal investigations originate from a fraud referral. 93% of the open criminal investigations are either from the US Attorney's Office, from another agency, self-developed by a special agent, or originate from Bank Secrecy Act data.

Once the suspicious activity is discovered, the IRS employee is supposed to contact their Fraud Enforcement Adviser (FEA). Many times, this does not happen because the employee wants to close the case and move on to an easier target.

A few times, I investigated potential criminal tax violations and discovered an outstanding tax balance due and collection activity on the defendant's tax transcript. Upon further review, I saw many instances where badges of fraud occurred during the IRS collection process, but when I reviewed the collection file, no contact with the FEA was made. My speculation is the revenue officer didn't know what they were looking at or ignored it.

The FEA is a trained IRS civil employee who knows what makes a good fraud referral. The FEA gives guidance to the IRS employee on how to develop the case further until it is ready for a possible criminal referral, such as gathering more financial documents, interviewing the taxpayer, etc. The most common guidance is to expand the tax years, get more documents, analyze more transactions, and investigate other nominee businesses or alter egos.

Flow of Badges of Fraud

There are two different thresholds when the IRS finds badges of fraud.

One is called an Indicator of Fraud. When the civil side starts investigating a taxpayer, an indicator of fraud may exist. The civil employee may see a company possibly being owned by a nominee, or personal living expenses being deducted as a business expense. For an indicator of fraud, it's not a problem for the IRS employee to continue gathering more information, including getting advice from the FEA on what information to pursue, how to get it, and how to analyze it.

Once the additional information reveals facts that point to a Firm Indication of Fraud, the civil agent is supposed to refer their findings for a possible criminal investigation. There is no bright line between an indicator of fraud and a firm indication of fraud; it is a matter of judgment. What the civil side cannot do is conduct a criminal tax investigation using its civil assessment and collection function. The federal courts won't allow a criminal tax investigation under the guise of a civil tax examination.

United States v. Tweel

United States v. Tweel is case law that every IRS criminal investigator knows because it is engrained into the minds of every IRS special agent in training. *Tweel* stated that a criminal investigation cannot be conducted under the guise of a civil examination.[6] Civil agents are not allowed to use deceit or trickery. They cannot lie to the taxpayers. So, if you ask the civil agent a flat-out question, such as "Did you refer the taxpayer to the Fraud Enforcement Adviser or to Criminal Investigation?" either they're going to keep their mouth shut or they're going to say, "No comment," but they can't say "no" if they did. They are not allowed to use trickery.

This is why the FEA position exists; it is a precaution to separate the civil employee from directly contacting the criminal investigator to further develop the case. To promote quality fraud referrals, IRS-CI does provide internal training to FEAs and civil employees about the characteristics of a good fraud referral.

Fraud Referral Process

If a firm indication of fraud is discovered worthy of evaluation by IRS-CI, there is a process to refer the case.[7] Before the fraud is officially referred for criminal investigation, the IRS employee gets an opinion from the FEA. This interaction is recorded in ICS (Integrated Collection System). ICS is the database whereby the revenue officer enters the collection activity. Contacting the FEA will not appear on tax transcripts so it won't be readily available unless you ask for certain files. If further development needs to be completed by the IRS civil employee, then that directive and results will be recorded in ICS as well. You will not know if the civil employee contacted a FEA for an opinion about a fraud referral from the tax transcripts; it will only be available in ICS files.

Audit sections have their own version. Because most of the fraud referrals come from collections, ICS will be discussed.

Once the civil employee, their supervisor, and FEA agree that a fraud referral is warranted, the file is submitted to IRS-CI for evaluation. This is detailed in

---

6. United States v. Tweel, 550 F.2d 297 (5th Cir. 1977)

7. Internal Revenue Service, U.S. Dep't of Treasury, Internal Revenue MANUAL § 9.4.1.5.1.3 (2021), available at https://www.irs.gov/irm/p art9/irm_09-004-001

IRM 9.4.1.5.1.3.2.[8] Ten days after that fraud referral is forwarded to IRS-CI, there is a conference between the civil side and the criminal side. This is also known as a "5-way" in IRS-CI lingo, where the special agent, his/her supervisor, the revenue officer/revenue agent, their supervisor, and the FEA, attend the same meeting and discuss the case.

What is Discussed During 5-Way Conference?

This meeting is where the civil employee sells their fraud referral to IRS-CI and IRS-CI has an opportunity to ask more questions. Before the meeting, IRS-CI will have general knowledge of the case, but probably won't have all the information for a proper evaluation. Some general questions that IRS-CI would be looking to answer include:

- What is the type of tax and estimated loss?

- What tax periods are you referring?

- Were tax returns solicited?

- Where are the original tax returns?

- Were attempts made to resolve the civil issues?

- Is the taxpayer just being obnoxious, or ignoring you?

- What makes IRS-CI the last resort to get this taxpayer's attention?

- Has the IRS taken prior actions involving the alleged offense for similar or past offenses?

- How old is this person?

---

8. Internal Revenue Service, U.S. Dep't of Treasury, Internal Revenue MANUAL § 9.4.1.5.1.3.2 (2021), available at https://www.irs.gov/irm/part9/irm_09-004-001

- Are they mentally capable of making business decisions now and during the tax fraud?

- Do they have physical problems?

- What are their health problems, if known?[9]

- What is the taxpayer's education?

- What does the taxpayer do for a living?

After the 5 Way Conference

After the 5-way conference, IRS-CI has 30 days to evaluate the fraud referral. Within those 30 days, IRS-CI can accept or deny the fraud referral. In my 20-year career, I have rejected only two fraud referrals. Those referrals were either not enough tax loss to be worthy to prosecute or not developed enough to show the willfulness necessary to generate a guilty verdict from a jury.

If the fraud referral is approved, the special agent will open a criminal tax investigation and request 914 control codes on the taxpayer's transcript. Internally, the 914 control codes show that there is an active criminal investigation on the taxpayer. This code puts the civil side on notice to cease further contact with the taxpayer, which means no more interviews, requests for documents, or mailing notices to the taxpayer. The 914 control code is tax and period specific. If a taxpayer later tries to file a tax return or make a tax payment for that tax and period, IRS-CI will get a notice from the civil side and the civil side will request guidance if they should accept the return or payment.

In most cases, IRS-CI will request the civil employee who submitted the fraud referral to be a cooperating agent with IRS-CI to assist in the criminal tax

---

9. IRS-CI will want to know about their health and mental conditions. IRS-CI does not expect the civil side to have medical records, but at least a general idea of the taxpayer's health.

investigation. This is done because the civil employee has intimate knowledge of the taxpayer, can assist in creating spreadsheets, and has the ability to decipher actions and reports conducted by the civil side. The cooperating agent could also be a witness in the grand jury, trial, or at sentencing. However, not all IRS civil employees want the possibility of taking the witness stand for cross examination.

Chapter 3

Evaluating a Fraud Referral

L et's look at how IRS-CI evaluates a potential criminal tax investigation. These criteria are not listed in order of importance but are criteria that IRS-CI takes into consideration throughout the investigation. The evaluation is not on a point system, but rather a scale. Not all weights are of equal value but they are all considered.

Greenberg v. United States

A major court case that IRS-CI has to consider is *Greenberg v. United States*.[1] If you meet an IRS-CI special agent and say that a *Greenberg* problem exists, they know exactly what you're talking about.

The burden of proof in a criminal investigation shifts from the taxpayer to the government. IRS-CI has to prove beyond a reasonable doubt in federal court that there's tax fraud. In a civil action, the burden of proof is on the taxpayer to have the receipt for a deduction. In criminal court, the burden of proof is on the government to show that the expense was not business but personal in nature.

---

1. Greenberg v. United States, 280 F.2d 472 (1st Cir. 1960)

In *Greenberg*, the court ruled that the special agent's testimony about the classification of checks as business or personal was inadmissible hearsay. A special agent cannot unilaterally categorize the purpose of payments or receipts. For example, if a check is made payable to the local utility company, a special agent might assume it is for the utility bill, but a special agent cannot testify that it was for the utility bill. In court, the utility company testifies that the check was for a utility bill or a taxpayer's bookkeeper will be called to do that.

Credible third-party witness testimony or corroborated admissions by the subject or the representative are required to categorize the purpose of payments or receipts. If there is a check made payable to cash, the burden of proof is on the government that the cash was not a business expense. Unless the special agent can prove that the cash was for personal use, the automatic presumption is that it is for business purposes.

The same dilemma exists regarding meal deductions and entertainment expenses. The automatic presumption is that each is a business expense, unless it can be proved otherwise.

Greenberg is one major reason that many tax cases are discontinued. For every relevant disbursement, the special agent is required to find and interview a witness that can discuss the meaning of the expense. The same goes for income as well. If checks are deposited into a bank account, IRS-CI has to interview the maker of the check. For either a deposit or disbursement, the government can spend an enormous amount of resources interviewing witnesses if the transactions are high volume and low amounts.

Administrative or Grand Jury?

IRS-CI can investigate a tax crime in two lanes: administrative or grand jury. One is called "administrative" because IRS-CI does have the authority to investigate criminal tax violations administratively. They do not need an Assistant United States Attorney (AUSA) at that time to conduct a tax investigation. They can issue a summons, just like a civil officer can issue a summons. IRS-CI uses the same form (Form 2039) to gather documents and compel testimony. If

IRS-CI does issue the summons, "Criminal Investigation" will be in the division section at the top of the summons.

There are pros and cons to an administrative investigation. IRS-CI is in charge of the investigation until it is referred for prosecution or elevated to a grand jury investigation. There is no need for an AUSA at that point in time. An administrative investigation is easier in some ways. The special agent doesn't have to wait for the AUSA to approve a grand jury subpoena. A summons can be issued on the spot. In an administrative case, I carried a blank summons, so I could complete it within minutes in front of the witness. Many times, in simple investigations, an administrative case can move more quickly.

In an administrative investigation, it is easier to return records to the civil side. A grand jury investigation restricts information found during a criminal tax investigation because of 6(e) material.[2] An administrative investigation allows full disclosure of information to the civil side, so if there is a need to share information, it can be completed seamlessly.

With an administrative investigation, the case agent only has two options: to investigate or close the case. There is no wiggle room for negotiating with the defendant about tax charges. This is important because only the Department of Justice can negotiate deals.

With a grand jury investigation, the US Attorney's Office is involved and the DOJ Tax Division is also aware of the investigation. The US Attorney's Office brings expertise and decision authority, like negotiating pleas and busting up conspiracies, that can move an investigation along.

A criminal tax defense attorney can persuade IRS-CI to close an administrative tax case easier than a grand jury tax investigation. With administrative investigations, the bar is lower for the case agent to open and to close the investigation. With a grand jury investigation, the US Attorney's Office typically has other non-tax violations in mind. The US Attorney's Office has an unwritten understanding with IRS-CI to not negotiate tax crimes away during plea negotiations. Because of IRS-CI's limited resources and the enormous time

---

2. Fed. R. Crim. P. 6(e)

that is required to investigate tax crimes, IRS-CI doesn't want to spend months or years in a grand jury case to later have the rug pulled out from under them at the last moment. For grand jury investigations, this could be good or bad for the defendant, depending on whether the tax violation is the better option.

If a criminal tax defense attorney wants to negotiate a plea deal for only tax violations, that is a better sale to the AUSA than for the AUSA to drop its tax charges. Of course, if there is a fatal flaw in the tax case, then the tax case will be closed.

I have sat in many pre-indictment conferences between the AUSA and the defense attorney, and the tax crimes have never been negotiated away. Many times, the tax violations created "checkmate" against the defendant. As a matter of fact, if there is some possibility that IRS-CI violations will not be indicted, the special agent has an obligation to let their superiors know. Once IRS is on the grand jury investigation, a criminal defense attorney can expect those violations to be pursued. IRS-CI is very picky about its statistics. If a case is closed late in the game, it gets scrutinized by upper management and sometimes phone calls are made between superiors about the use of IRS-CI in grand jury cases.

Tax Loss

Tax loss is how large the expected loss will be at sentencing. Before an investigation is started, the tax loss is very fluid, but based on the volume of money at stake, the special agent should have a general idea of the tax loss. The tax loss has a large impact on the decision, because tax loss drives the sentencing. The sentencing guidelines for tax violations are found in section 2T1.1 of the United States Sentencing Commission Guidelines Manual.[3] IRS-CI isn't interested in the sentencing range of probation, so the loss needs to be near or above that range for IRS-CI to pursue an investigation.

Tax loss can affect sentencing to different degrees depending on the judicial district. In New York City, tax loss needs to be higher than Asheville, North

---

3. U.S. Sentencing Comm'n, Guidelines Manual § 2T1.1 (2021)

Carolina for active prison time. Every IRS-CI office knows the threshold that judges are using for active prison time. As part of IRS-CI's mission statement, IRS-CI actively seeks tax cases that will create a deterrence effect in the general public. IRS-CI wants publicity for active prison time for defendants. Press releases showing no active prison time are not the type of publicity that IRS-CI is seeking. You will rarely see a press release for probation on a tax violation; it is not a story that IRS-CI wants to be told.

IRS-CI's phrase for a low tax loss not worth the time to prosecute is called "not meeting LEM." LEM is short for Law Enforcement Manual. LEM is a non-public document for IRS-CI special agents to give guidance for tax prosecutions. I have read it and there is nothing of interest in it to discuss because the recommendations are vague. If you tell a special agent that his estimated tax loss won't meet LEM, he will know exactly what you mean.

Venue

An IRS-CI special agent rarely works an investigation outside their commuting area. As an internal joke, one long-time employee stated that outside an hour driving distance the chance of a criminal investigation diminishes drastically, which has some truth to it. Special agents have personal lives, family responsibilities, and financial constraints. If a special agent is paying for childcare, is it really worth it being hours away from home to investigate a tax violation? Is having a case take them away from home more often worth the headache of not being at dinner with the family? Unless special circumstances are present, the cases are worked locally. Venue plays a vital importance for efficiency. If venue is not in the same area, most likely it will be sent to the district where it can be charged. With the number of special agents in decline over the last 10 years, there are some remote areas that IRS-CI never touches.

Medical History

As mentioned in the 5-way conference section of this book, medical history is important to the IRS-CI determination whether to pursue an investigation.

- Is the person capable of going to prison?

- Is criminal willfulness affected by the medical condition?

- Is the judge going to have sympathy for their medical condition?

Medical history usually comes into play if the defendant's life expectancy is short or the medical condition will cause unnecessary strain on the prison's health-care system.

Age

Is this person 18 or 85? If someone is 85, IRS-CI is probably not going to do so much with them. If someone is 44, the defendant can spend some time in prison.

Notoriety

What is the notoriety of the taxpayer? Is this person an elected official, judge, or prominent person in a position of trust?

IRS-CI will investigate a lower tax loss to make an example out of a public figure. The goal of IRS-CI is to make examples out of people who are not complying with tax laws. Public figures will receive more attention from the media and lose their public office, which is a deterrent to the general public and hopefully to other public figures. This is especially true for suspicious income, such as possible bribes or kickbacks.

Education

As mentioned in the 5-way conference section of this book, IRS-CI will also look at the education of the violator. Is the person a CPA? Is the person an attorney? Doctor? Doctors are well known to earn high incomes but frequently have limited business knowledge, whereas the CPA really has no excuse for violating general tax law. A person with no high school education has a lower chance of knowing tax law than a business college graduate. That chance is even lower when the defendant is not originally from the United States and never graduated from high school.

Filing Compliance

Is there a pattern of noncompliance? Is the person committing tax crimes for one year or over five years? A one-year tax case has too many problems to overcome. One problem is proving willfulness, and the other is that the tax loss is typically too low to justify pursuing the investigation. Showing a pattern of non-compliance is directly related to the willfulness element in criminal tax statutes, and it has jury appeal. A jury can understand that years of bad behavior show willfulness.

Legal or Illegal Source

Is this a legal or illegal source of income? A legal source would be income as a plumber, doctor, CPA, etc. An illegal source would income from selling illegal drugs, fraud, embezzlement, Ponzi scheme, etc.

If it's a legal source case, then IRS-CI will most likely take the case, because only IRS-CI can investigate tax crimes. If it's an illegal source case, IRS-CI will measure if the tax case brings any value to the prosecution of the illegal activity that created the income. It may be better suited for another agency to take. Many times, IRS-CI is used by AUSAs to investigate tax crimes on unreported income from illegal activities because it is easier to prove the tax violation than the illegal activity.

Disposition of Funds

Where did the money go to if it didn't pay for the taxes? Did it pay for personal living expenses? Is it paying for the wife's cancer treatment?

This goes directly to jury appeal. IRS-CI isn't interested in a trial where the jury is only told to "Put this defendant in prison because the tax evasion is $100,000." The jury wants to know where the money went. If they discover that it paid for the spouse's cancer treatment, that won't sell very well.

Disposition of funds will sell if the funds paid for the family to attend Disneyland every year and maintained a couple of girlfriends. I've had this type of case before. Instead of paying the taxes, the defendant lives a lavish lifestyle, such as nice vacations, multiple homes, boats, planes, etc. That's going to sell to a jury.

Availability of Records

Are the records available? Banks usually keep financial records up to 6 years. Anything past that date has a low probability of record retention. Some banks are located in foreign countries which do not comply with document requests. Is it reasonable for books and records to exist, and if so then where? In addition, do the credit applications report a different amount than the tax returns? Prosecutors love to show a credit application that is materially different than the tax return.

Search Warrant Needed?

Is a search warrant needed? Are the pertinent records available at a business or residence? Is probable cause reasonably available to get a search warrant approved? If the key evidence in the case can only be reasonably obtained through a search warrant, IRS-CI must evaluate very quickly before evidence is moved or destroyed.

Commingling

Is the defendant commingling business and personal living expenses? Commingling is a very common occurrence for self-employed business owners. Most frequent is abuse of the corporate credit card, which is used to purchase personal living expenses. Can IRS-CI separate what's business and what's personal? Remember, *Greenberg* is important here. Somebody with personal knowledge has to testify to facts showing that the disbursement at Victoria's Secret was personal in nature, rather than hearsay conclusions about the nature of the purchase. It is a good assumption that a purchase at Victoria's Secret would be personal in nature, but the government needs a witness to prove the nature of the purchase.

Defendant's Actions or Statements

The best summary I created as a special agent was a timeline of actions taken by the IRS and the defendant's responses. When the IRS initiated an action, the defendant responded by hiding their income or assets. The timeline showed various steps the taxpayer took during the collection activity. For example, when the defendant filed a bankruptcy petition stopping IRS collection activity, she had purchased a boat using a nominee name two days prior. Sometimes the defendant creates their own problems by using social media to brag about their wealth or crimes. If the defendant has a social media presence, expect it to be part of the investigation.

Reliance Defense

The reliance defense is when the defendant received bad advice or the tax return preparer was negligent in preparing the tax return. Negligence by the return preparer could include not asking the right questions or making errors on the tax return. IRS-CI special agents will interview the return preparer and ask for the supporting documents and communication between the return preparer and the defendant. In many cases, the defendant withheld information from the return preparer. Sometimes a reliance defense occurs if another person (e.g., girlfriend) is the point of contact for tax matters between the defendant and the return preparer. If the defendant relied on the girlfriend to compile and deliver financial records to the return preparer, then who is at fault?

In the beginning of the investigation, the special agent will interview the defendant and return preparer, usually within days of each other to gauge any potential reliance defense.

Language Barrier

Language barrier is a huge obstacle to overcome in an investigation for two reasons. First, if the defendant's foreign language is used in communication with other key witnesses, then the IRS has to find a special agent that speaks that language to assist in the investigation. That same agent has to interview those witnesses and prepare the memorandums of interview. This is a huge drain on resources, rendering the case agent leading an investigation more as a spectator than a primary agent. Second, the return preparer most likely speaks the same foreign language, which can be difficult because of technical issues in United States tax law. Some words or phrases don't translate very well.

In my career, I have never experienced a language barrier be overcome by IRS-CI. Spanish isn't as much of a problem in Miami and other parts of the country such as southern Texas, because there are special agents who speak the language. Outside of those areas, particularly in the southeastern United States, I only knew one Spanish speaking special agent within three states.

Hot Topic

IRS-CI has a list of priorities for tax compliance, which is published every year. Currently hot topics are cryptocurrency, payroll taxes, and foreign bank accounts. An investigation into those topics will get attention.

Current Tax Compliance

The IRS wants tax compliance. IRS-CI is only part of the tax enforcement. IRS-CI is the last gasp effort to get taxpayers into compliance. Before spending any resources opening a criminal investigation, IRS-CI wants to know: has the taxpayer changed his/her ways in tax compliance? IRS-CI is not interested in opening an investigation into a taxpayer who is actively pursuing compliance. There is no jury appeal if an investigation is open on a compliant taxpayer. Furthermore, there is less of an appeal for a judge to give the defendant an active prison sentence. It's easier to open a criminal investigation if the person hasn't complied for 10 years, got caught by the civil side, and continued to thwart the government's lawful efforts to collect the proper taxes. If the taxpayer changed his ways prior to IRS-CI's involvement, where is the incentive to put the person in prison?

Compliance is not a "get out of jail free" card if the taxpayer complies only after a criminal investigation has started, but I have never seen a fraud referral where the taxpayer is actively trying to comply and a criminal investigation started anyways. To the contrary, I had many conversations with upper management where they would agree that they were not interested in pursuing a criminal investigation into someone who was actively trying to resolve their civil tax obligations. I have heard many civil tax attorneys wring their hands over an audit or collection activity that could possibly be a fraud referral. My advice is to be proactive: file the missing tax returns, amend the inaccurate tax returns, and start making payments on the tax liability. The only way to get into further trouble is to file another false return, which is doubling down on stupid. The chance of a fraud referral being accepted by IRS-CI is about zero when the taxpayer is doing the right thing.

Chapter 4

Common Criminal
Tax Statutes

W hen IRS-CI evaluates a criminal investigation, the evidence must fit the violation. The best resource on the various nuances of these elements of tax crimes is the Tax Crimes Handbook[1] published by IRS Office of Chief Counsel. It is the guidebook that IRS-CI uses in proving the elements of the crimes.

I am not going into detail on the various possible criminal tax violations. But I will mention the most common statutes:

---

1. Internal Revenue Service, U.S. Dep't of Treasury, Tax Crimes Handbook (2009)

Title 26, 7201 (Tax Evasion)

Elements of the Offense:[2]

    1. An attempt to evade or defeat a tax or the payment of a tax;

    2. An additional tax due and owing; and,

    3. Willfulness.

This violation is approached two ways: a tax is already on the books and IRS is trying to collect, or the defendant is trying to not have the tax properly assessed. For most fraud referrals, the tax is already assessed and the IRS is trying to collect it, but the defendant is making attempts to have his income or assets hidden from the IRS.

Title 26, 7202 (Willful Failure Or To Pay Over Tax)

Elements of the Offense:[3]

    1. Duty to collect, and/or to truthfully account for and pay over;

    2. Failure to collect, or truthfully account for and pay over; and

    3. Willfulness.

This statute is commonly used for unpaid payroll taxes. It would apply when a person has collected taxes from their employees' wages but did not turn those taxes over to the United States Treasury. It would also apply to those employers who pay their employees in cash and don't withhold taxes as required. Both situations would fit under this statute.

---

2. I.R.C. § 7201 (2022)

3. I.R.C. § 7202 (2022)

Title 26, 7206(1) (Filing a False Tax Return)

Elements of the Offense:[4]

1. Making and subscribing a return, statement, or other document which was false as to a material matter;

2. The return, statement, or other document contained a written declaration that it was made under the penalties of perjury;

3. The maker did not believe the return, statement, or other document to be true and correct as to every material matter; and,

4. The maker falsely subscribed to the return, statement, or other document willfully, with the specific intent to violate the law.

This statute is commonly used for tax returns that have a false material item, but the tax loss is more difficult to prove. Not reporting foreign bank accounts and foreign assets would be an example of a false material item. Also, this statute is commonly used for unreported gross receipts when the special agent can prove that the sales were materially unreported. The special agent then isn't required to prove the tax loss during the trial, but only that the gross receipts were materially inaccurate.

Notice this statute targets a return that is filed under penalties of perjury, so many tax forms filed with the IRS would fit under this statute because most have a jurat. Defining materiality is up to the courts.

---

4. I.R.C. § 7206(1) (2022)

Title 26, 7206(2) (Aiding or Assisting the Preparation of a False or Fraudulent Document)

Elements of the Offense:[5]

1. The defendant aided or assisted in, or procured, counseled, or advised the preparation or presentation of a return, affidavit, claim, or other document which involved a matter arising under the Internal Revenue laws;

2. The return, affidavit, claim, or other document was fraudulent or false as to a material matter; and,

3. Willfulness

This statute is commonly used for return preparers who are preparing false tax returns. It is also for those who help in filing false tax returns even if they did not prepare it. Such individuals could be those who prepared false documents or advised how to file a false tax return.

---

5. I.R.C. § 7206(2) (2022)

Chapter 5

Ways to Prevent A Fraud Referral

A fter looking at the facts and you think a client may be susceptible to a fraud referral, here some steps that you can take to help your client through the process:

File a Form 2848 (Power of Attorney)

File a Form 2848 (Power of Attorney) so that the IRS can disclose tax information to you. File the Form 2848 with the IRS per the form's instructions and give a copy of the form to the revenue officer if they are assigned to the case.

The Power of Attorney (POA) is entity, type of tax, and tax period specific. It is best to use a 10-year period of time. The type of tax should be income and payroll (if your client is an employer). If the taxpayer controls various entities such as businesses, trusts, etc., then a POA for each entity will be required.

Get Current Tax Information

Request current tax information on your client for the years under investigation. With a POA, you have the right to this tax information from the IRS under U.S.C. Title 26 section 6103(c).[1] The revenue officer should be able to get you this information. When you contact the IRS civil employee, let them know that you are trying to ascertain the problem and avenues to get your client into compliance. The IRS is trying to receive unfiled tax returns, determine how they are going to get paid, set up some type of payment plan, and then close the case. The quicker this is resolved, the better it is for your client.

Hire an Expert

Some tax attorneys excel in dealing with the IRS. But as you already know, not all attorneys are created equal. You may need to hire someone who has experience in dealing with the IRS in these high-stress situations. Expanding your network to include CPAs, Enrolled Agents, and former IRS employees will pay dividends in getting clients into tax compliance. At times, the non-attorneys may be less expensive, and just as capable to assist in resolving the problem.

Do Your Homework

Don't trust the taxpayer to tell you everything or know everything. Look at the pattern, years, amounts, changing companies, previous suspicious activities, etc. If the collection activity is from unpaid payroll taxes, you need to have a serious conversation with your client. Where did the money go instead of paying payroll taxes? Does it keep the business afloat? Unpaid payroll tax is considered theft by the United States Congress, but the tax violation does not have jury appeal when the taxes are used to keep the business solvent. However, if it paid for large wages or for personal living expenses, that does have jury appeal. You need to ask who got the benefit of the unpaid payroll taxes.

---

1. I.R.C. § 6103(c) (2022)

Don't Let the Client Be Interviewed

If you believe that a criminal investigation could arise from your client's actions, then don't let the client be interviewed. If the civil side wants to talk to your client and you think they may have potential criminal problems, then request a list of questions and offer a written response. Taxpayers say the weirdest things during interviews. They either lie or admit wrongdoings.

If the non-compliance relates to unpaid payroll taxes, the revenue officer will request to interview your client to determine if your client qualifies as a "responsible party" to assess the Trust Fund Recovery Penalty (TFRP). The revenue officer will use a Form 4180 (Report of Interview with Individual Relative to Trust Fund Recovery Penalty or Personal Liability for Excise Taxes) as their guide to prove or disprove if the TFRP should be assessed. Again, if you believe that there is potential for a fraud referral, don't let the taxpayer be interviewed. Any statements made by your client can be used against them later in a criminal tax investigation. By default, if an interview is never completed, the revenue officer will assess the TFRP anyways. In many cases, the business owner will be assessed the TFRP. The completion of Form 4180 by the revenue officer would be a formality. I cannot stress enough that you should hire a professional who is experienced in tax representation because unpaid payroll tax can cause a substantial amount of financial harm and is a hot compliance topic for IRS-CI.

Many times, the question arises if the client should attend a meeting with the IRS and plead the 5th Amendment against self-incrimination. In my opinion, I would rather have the client not be interviewed than be in an interview and plead the 5th Amendment. Invoking silence during a civil examination adds suspicion.

Pay the Tax Bill and File the Amended Tax Return

Paying the tax liability doesn't absolve the taxpayer, but it does lessen the motivation for a criminal tax investigation. There may be penalties, but it will be cheaper than a criminal investigation. If compliance is complete before IRS-CI gets the fraud referral, where is the motivation to start a criminal investigation? The government does not want to waste resources on an investigation with a high likelihood of an acquittal or sympathy from a judge at sentencing.

If amended returns need to be filed, then file them before a criminal referral is made. There is a possibility that a "5th Amendment return" can be filed, but that return must have enough information to determine a tax due.[2] I have never seen these type of tax returns, but they can exist.

Turn Over Records

If your client has business records that have been summonsed, then turn them over. If the records don't exist, don't have the client recreate the records unless a professional is hired. No document is better than an inaccurate document.

Here's what happens when the client tries to recreate records. The civil side requests documents, and the taxpayer thinks he is doing a favor by preparing a document that was requested. If the document is not complete or incorrect, the civil side believes that it's an affirmative act of evasion. As part of the fraud referral, the civil employee brings that suspicious document to IRS-CI and makes a point that it was an effort to evade taxes. That's not what you want.

The IRS has a right to request books and records. If the books and records are on QuickBooks or a similar bookkeeping software, the IRS can require those files in that format.[3] However, if the IRS asks for electronic copies of the books and records, only give them what is requested and not the whole file. Otherwise, the client is opening themselves up to more fishing expeditions. Don't give a decade of records if they're not asking for it.

---

2. United States v. Sullivan, 274 U.S. 259 (1927); Garner v. United States, 424 U.S. 648 (1976); United States v. Barnes, 604 F.2d 121 (2d Cir. 1979).

3. Rev. Rul. 71-20, 1971-1 CB 392

Craft Your Excuse, If Applicable

If you have a good excuse for the lack of compliance, then make your case. This also helps prevent a criminal investigation. Some acceptable reasons are:

- the spouse was in the hospital during that period of time

- a child had medical emergencies, which created lack of attention to filing requirements

- the taxpayer was going through drug problems and rehab

- the taxpayer has been medically diagnosed with depression

- records were destroyed in a fire or flood

Whatever the reasonable excuse, provide documentation to the civil employee, even if it only covers part of the non-compliance.

During the 5-way conference, medical and health problems are part of the conversation; so are the availability of records. If the civil side already has documentation for the reasonable excuse, IRS-CI has limited reasons to open a criminal investigation. Remember that questions are asked about health, mental problems and availability of records. If IRS-CI discovers that the civil side knew about these problems and didn't disclose it, that's a case killer in my opinion. IRS-CI is interested in slam dunks and not into second guessing why they weren't told about reasonable excuses.

Social Media

Keep the client's activity off social media, like Instagram and Facebook. Pictures tell a thousand words, and juries will remember pictures better than verbal testimony or statements. With the prevalence of social media, your client should temporarily suspend posting social media. Some attorneys question if removing social media pictures or deleting the accounts can be construed as evidence tampering. I have no opinion on this action. But I do know that IRS employees will go to social media to look at your client's lifestyle. Some of the best evidence for jury appeal has come from the defendant's social media accounts, including a video of the taxpayer bragging about his tax violations and pictures of vacations in foreign countries funded by unpaid payroll taxes.

Conduct Tax Compliance Triage

Most clients don't have deep pockets and hiring attorneys and CPAs to solve their tax problems is expensive. If a tax compliance triage is necessary, I would recommend that the recent years be fixed first, then go backwards. This is for two main reasons: First, if a fraud referral is a possibility, then having your client in compliance for the most recent years shows good faith; second, the IRS civil side usually won't go back further than six years for tax compliance.[4] The Internal Revenue Manual policy statement entitled *Delinquent returns—enforcement of filing requirements*, discusses delinquent returns and the enforcement of filing requirements. The more time that passes, the better the chances that the older years will never be examined.

Have An Adult Conversation with Your Client

I will step on a soapbox for a moment. The actions that create a potential fraud referral can be stopped. Some taxpayers are arrogant enough to believe that they are bulletproof because they have escaped scrutiny for their behavior for years and maybe decades. I have a podcast called the Fraud Fighter Podcast. In some of the episodes, I interviewed AUSAs who are responsible for seizing assets to pay criminal judgments. The consequences of a federal conviction and judgment in federal court are tremendous because the power to collect is far-reaching and quick. This is not state court where some states have limited collection abilities.

---

4. Internal Revenue Service, U.S. Dept of Treasury, Internal Revenue Manual § 1.2.1.6.18 (2006), available at https://www.irs.gov/irm/part1/irm_01-002-001

The bottom line is that if your client does not solve their potential fraud referral, the consequences will be severe and dramatic. Here would be my talking points if your client was in front of me:

- If a fraud referral is successful and IRS-CI takes this to court, the United States has over a 90% conviction rate. Those are not good odds.

- When the judgment is ordered by a federal judge, then active prison time will most likely follow.

- The order for restitution will be for all the taxes that were owed, which could include relevant conduct that exceeds the current civil problem they are experiencing.

- Federal attorneys and the IRS will have the authority to seize and sell assets to pay for the restitution.

- The restitution order is for 20 years for the federal government to collect.[5] The Department of Justice can request to extend it after 20 years.

- When they leave prison, the judge will require restitution payments to stay out of prison.

- Under supervised release, they will be asking permission to travel and will be subject to searches by the United States Probation Office.

- The restitution in the judgment order cannot be discharged in bankruptcy. They are stuck with this for two decades.

- Any reputation they enjoy now will be tarnished because they will become a felon, which mean loss of livelihood, not possessing a firearm, not voting, etc.

---

5. 18 U.S.C. § 3613(b) (2022)

- Their relationship with family and friends will be strained, with possible divorce and child custody battles.

- The legal fees and litigation support fees to defend them will be high.

Or

- They can file those missing tax returns, correctly amend the tax returns, and get on a payment plan.

- If they are too poor to pay their taxes, the IRS will suspend collections for two years and then re-evaluate their ability to pay.

- The collection of civil taxes has a 10-year statute of limitations, after assessment. In some cases, those taxes can be discharged in bankruptcy and can be negotiated for "pennies on the dollar."

- They can stay out of prison, keep their reputation, and have their life back once the dust settles with the collection activity. It is not pleasant, but I would rather wake up each morning in my bed than in a bunk bed behind bars.

- Hiring professionals to fix civil tax problems is cheaper than hiring professionals to represent them in federal criminal court.

I think I would take the compliance route. I am stepping down from the soapbox now.

Chapter 6

Signs of a Potential or Successful Criminal Fraud Referral

L et's assume that your client has all the characteristics of a fraud referral and you don't know where the IRS is heading. What are the signs of a pending fraud referral?

The most common reasons to believe that a criminal fraud referral is being considered are:

- the revenue officer is expanding his tax years under review.

- the client is no longer receiving notices.

- the revenue officer suddenly is not answering emails or returning phone calls.

- the revenue officer is obtaining more bank and credit card information.

- the revenue officer is asking more questions as to "why."

But how would you know quickly if the referral was successful?

To verify a successful fraud referral, the first step is to get a copy of the taxpayer's transcripts for the years that are under investigation. If the transcript has a 914 control code, then IRS-CI has officially opened the investigation. I have heard of some transcripts that were redacted by IRS. A redaction (near the date of the collection activity) could be assumed to be a criminal tax investigation.

The 914 control code stops civil right in its tracks. Remember the *Tweel* case? To prevent any potential *Tweel* problems, civil will stop contacting your client and any representative. No more notices are in the mail. There is no more contact with the taxpayer.

Any tax return or payment associated with the 914 control code will be suspended. The civil side will contact the IRS-CI case agent to request advice on how to proceed if there is civil activity. The tax return or payment will not be posted unless IRS-CI approves. In addition, if you contact the civil side on the phone, they will not discuss the case with you about compliance when a 914 control code is in place.

When IRS-CI has approved the fraud referral, then IRS-CI will develop a strategy for the next step. This could be a search warrant, undercover operation, covertly taking the client's trash, surveillance, etc. If there is a pending search warrant, it will take typically a month or two to develop probable cause, write the search warrant affidavit, have it reviewed by various attorneys, have the warrant issued by a federal magistrate, and ultimately execute the warrant.

I have never experienced this situation, but if you discover early that IRS-CI has taken the case, but IRS-CI hasn't officially been in contact with you or your client, it wouldn't be a bad idea to contact the local IRS-CI office to ask for the case agent's name and open a dialog. Have a POA in hand before you make the contact, because it will expedite the conversation.

During that time, notify them that you do not want them to contact your client. This may stop them from any enforcement activity. (I can't promise that it will or won't.) This is unchartered territory for me. I have never heard of an attorney discovering a criminal tax investigation once it was opened and prior to any enforcement activity, but it would be worth the phone call.

Another characteristic of a criminal fraud referral is IRS conducting interviews with two agents. IRS-CI often interviews key witnesses with two agents. Their business card will have "Criminal Investigation" on it, and so will the summons if issued. During an administrative criminal investigation, the defendant will be read his or her rights. If it is a grand jury tax investigation, the reading of those rights will be at the discretion of the AUSA.

Chapter 7

Typical Fraud Referral

E very criminal fraud referral that I've ever received from the civil side had these similar characteristics:

The taxpayer owes a substantial amount of money, typically over $100,000. The revenue officer is assigned to solicit the unfiled tax returns and to interview the taxpayer to determine what assets and income are available to pay the tax liability.

The revenue officer interviews the taxpayer, and during the interview the Form 433A (Collection Information Statement for Wage Earners and Self-Employed Individuals) is completed, which lists the taxpayer's assets and income. A Form 433A is a collection information statement that is signed under penalty of perjury. Once completed and signed, the Form 433A is missing substantial assets and income earned by the taxpayer.

Based on the taxpayer's primary residence and vehicles, the taxpayer appears to be living a lavish lifestyle, and it is inconsistent with the Form 433A that the taxpayer signed. Any unfiled tax returns continue to be unfiled despite promises made by the taxpayer to file those missing tax returns. Because of the inconsistency of the taxpayer's lifestyle compared to the Form 433A and possible other previous tax returns, the revenue officer starts to summons bank statements. In those bank statements, the volume of deposits is greater than expected.

The revenue officer then finds evidence of credit card payments. The revenue officer continues his research into the credit card payments. He notices that the taxpayer appears to be commingling business and personal living expenses and also notices that the credit card payments are made from an unknown bank account. The newly discovered bank account is summonsed and analyzed. This new bank account is under a nominee name. In addition, car loan and mortgage applications show income greater than the taxpayer's tax returns and recently completed Form 433A.

If it is an unpaid payroll tax situation, the taxpayer has a pattern of opening and closing businesses but continues to operate in the same location, have the same employees, and stay in the same industry. When the taxpayer is caught for unpaid payroll taxes, the taxpayer starts another business and continues the same pattern of not turning over payroll taxes. The revenue officer finds that assets are discovered to be placed in another family member's name, so the taxpayer does not own the business but still appears to be operating it.

If there is a follow-up interview by the revenue officer with the taxpayer, the taxpayer continues to promise compliance, but does not comply with the revenue officer's requests. It is also not uncommon for the taxpayer to lie to the revenue officer when the revenue officer offers evidence that rebuts the taxpayer's previous statements.

Instead of fixing the problems, the taxpayer continues a lifestyle of non-compliance, leaving the revenue officer with the realization that no matter what he does, the taxpayer is going to continue doing the same thing.

The taxpayer hasn't learned his lesson about compliance. He is not doing what he is supposed to do and continues to put his thumb in the eye of the IRS.

This is not a driver traveling 56 mph in a 55-mph zone. This is similar to the guy speeding on the highway doing 80 mph in a 55-mph zone, weaving in and out of traffic, throwing beer cans out the window, and showing everybody his middle finger. Without IRS-CI's intervention, he will not be stopped. It is so egregious that the judge and jury will understand why the criminal charges were brought, with the hopes that the general public will thank IRS-CI for doing its job.

After months or years of trying to get the taxpayer in compliance, the revenue officer submits the fraud referral which is accepted by IRS-CI. A good fraud referral is easily accepted.

When IRS-CI gets the case, whether from a fraud referral or another source, there are certain steps that you can take to help your client as much as possible in the investigation/pre-indictment stage, which is covered in the next chapter.

Chapter 8

When the Client is Under a Criminal Tax Investigation

O nce your client is under criminal investigation or you think they are under criminal investigation, there are certain steps you can take. It won't matter if the case was a fraud referral, because these steps are universal in a pre-indictment stage. Furthermore, as you progress through this book you will notice that there is some overlap in techniques and tactics, so bear with me if some items are repeated.

Here are the steps that you need to take; the first five should be in order:

File a Power of Attorney

File a Form 2848 (Power of Attorney) so that the IRS can disclose tax information to you. File the Form 2848 with the IRS per the form's instructions, and give a copy of the form to the special agent for their files.

Never assume that the special agent will file the form. That way if there is any reason to contact the civil side directly, then the POA will already be filed. When you give a copy to the special agent, write "copy" or "already filed" on the top so there is no misunderstanding. This will also be needed because in any discussion you have with IRS Criminal Tax Counsel or another IRS-CI employee, those employees will want a copy in their hands so they are not committing a disclosure violation talking to you.

If it is a grand jury investigation, many federal prosecutors and special agents take the position that no POA is needed because Title 26 U.S.C. section 6103(h) allows special agents to discuss tax information to criminal defense attorneys. But don't be surprised if it is asked by the IRS-CI special agent.

Key Takeaway: File a Form 2848 with the IRS so that you can receive tax information.

Hire an Expert

Under a *Kovel* agreement,[1] hire a CPA or expert who is experienced with criminal tax investigations, preferably someone who was a former IRS-CI special agent. I cannot stress enough that an expert can help you craft any reasonable arguments in persuading IRS-CI to close the investigation. There are very few criminal tax experts out there worth hiring. The same expert can help interview key witnesses to determine the best strategy for your client's circumstances. Get as much information to the expert as possible initially to start the process. The expert should be able to review the tax transcripts and financial information to determine if there is a potential *Greenberg* problem, *Tweel* problem, reliance defense, or some other reasonable explanation for the defendant. Hiring an expert won't change the facts, but does help craft your response.

If the investigation becomes an indictment, your expert can assist you in the discovery, trial, and sentencing stage. It is well worth the price on the front end to have an expert in your corner, especially someone with IRS experience. The transcripts from the IRS are not easy to read or comprehend. Even veteran IRS employees need assistance in understanding these documents.

---

1. United States v. Kovel, 296 F.2d 918 (2d Cir. 1961)

Key Takeaway: Hire an expert to assist you in evaluating the criminal investigation

Get Current Tax Information

Request current tax information on your client for the years under investigation. With a Power of Attorney, you have the right to this tax information from the IRS under U.S.C. Title 26, section 6103(c).[2] In addition, under IRM section 9.3.1.3.11, IRS-CI is to turn over tax information from their files.[3] I will give you a heads up about this request. If you ask for this information, expect their ears to perk up, because in my 20 years of experience, no attorney has ever asked for this information up front. In addition, when you ask for certain tax transcripts, which I will give you below, the IRS special agent, their supervisor, and the whole local office will know that you are very experienced in dealing in criminal tax violations. Why? Because no attorney asks for this information, and if they did, I am 100% certain that your request will be made known throughout the office because it will be so unusual. They are going to know that you have experts on your team, which in my opinion puts them on notice that this isn't going to be easy for them.

If this is a grand jury investigation, the AUSA already has a copy of the tax information because it is part of the package that IRS-CI forwarded to the US Attorney's Office. It may be commingled with other information that you won't be privy to, but those documents are there. I have found that AUSAs are open to turning over information that you have a right to according to law during the pre-indictment stage.

At a minimum, you should request the following:

---

2. I.R.C. § 6103(c) (2022)

3. Internal Revenue Service, U.S. Dep't of Treasury, Internal Revenue Manual § 9.3.1.3.11 (2015), available at https://www.irs.gov/irm/part9/irm_09-003-001.

IRPTRL - This transcript shows third-party information that was filed with the IRS, such as Forms 1099, 1098, W-2, etc. This is important because it shows all possible leads of assets and income, including foreign assets.

INOLES - This transcript is a summary of the name, address, and SSN/ITIN cross references. If there are other businesses associated with your client, this may be helpful.

MFTRA -C - This is the master transcript that will show all transactions associated with the account, such as tax filings, notices, penalties, interest, payments, etc. This transcript shows all activity on the account.

Tax Return Transcript - This is an English version of the transcript similar to the MFTRA, but it doesn't have all the information that a MFTRA will have. This a readable version that will be helpful in getting an overview of what is happening.

Copies of Original Tax Returns - If the tax returns were electronically filed, this will be a printout similar to the actual tax return. If it is a paper return, then you will want a copy of the paper return. You will not get the original return.

If a Fraud Referral, a Copy of the Civil File - The civil file should be in the hands of IRS-CI if there is a fraud referral, but not always because some special agents may not ask for it.

Key Takeaway: Getting current tax information is vital to understanding the framework of the allegations that your client is facing.

Is this Administrative or Grand Jury?

Find out if the case is administrative or grand jury. If a case is an administrative investigation, you can get an idea of where it originated based on its characteristics. If the defendant has a cash lifestyle it was more likely opened from a Bank Secrecy Act source. If the defendant lives in a nice house and qualified for the Earned Income Tax Credit, then the source was data mining of taxpayers living in expensive zip codes. Most of these types of cases are opened administratively first. It's important because these are more fishing expeditions, and special agents have less skin in the game initially.

A grand jury investigation is opened for two main reasons. First, the AUSA has invited IRS-CI to the investigation because it needs IRS-CI's expertise and believes that a tax fraud case needs to be pursued. Or secondly, IRS-CI believes that the case is too complex, such as a conspiracy, to handle in an administrative investigation. A grand jury investigation is harder to discontinue, but it will allow you to have an open dialog with the AUSA, which can be helpful.

Key Takeaway: Finding the reason the case was opened can assist you in determining the government's level of dedication to its investigation.

Reliance Defense

Check if there is a reliance defense. Interview the bookkeeper or return preparer who would be responsible for completing the filed tax returns.

- Was this an honest mistake?

- What documents were given to the return preparer?

- Did the return preparer review the tax return with the client before it was filed?

You will need to know how information flowed from the defendant to the return preparer. In larger CPA firms, the true return preparer is different than the signed, paid return preparer. The true return preparer will be a lower-paid professional, but the signature will be from a partner who relied on the employee for an accurate return.

Ask your client if they hired someone even if the tax returns were not filed. If the return was never filed, but the client hired a return preparer, then IRS-CI may never know about them, unless they find a check leading to that preparer.

I had one investigation where the defendant hired a CPA firm to prepare his personal tax returns, but the tax returns were never filed with the IRS. I discovered those returns when the defendant used those returns to open a business account. Who was at fault for not filing the returns? Some CPAs file tax returns for their clients; others do not.

Also determine if the return preparer was at fault for not doing his or her job. Did they ask the right questions from the defendant? Sometimes the return preparer asked for more information, but the defendant never turned it over to them, leaving the return preparer to not file on time. Better yet, the return preparer knew that information was missing but filed it anyways. I had one case where the CPA prepared and recommended a tax return for his client to sign that was not accurate, but justified that the defendant can file an amended tax return later when more information came in. The amended tax return was never filed, so I was left with a false tax return that I could not prosecute. Needless to say, that return preparer would not have been a great witness for the prosecution.

As a side note, not all special agents have the same background in tax return preparation. Some were former IRS civil employees. Some came from the banking industry. Some were auditors in large CPA firms. Not many were CPAs in public accounting that prepared tax returns for a living prior to becoming special agents; that background in tax preparation is rare. I say this because without that return preparation background, I have noticed that special agents don't conduct a full and complete interview on return preparers. Furthermore, the special agent is supposed to trace what the return preparer received from the defendant to the tax return, and then compare that tax return to reality. In almost every case, I found mistakes by the return preparer. Some were minor, but others were not.

Key Takeaway: By following the flow of tax information, a reliance defense is the most effective way to cast reasonable doubt in an investigation.

Follow IRS Leads

If it's an administrative investigation, follow the financial breadcrumb trail. In an administrative investigation, the IRS sends notices to the taxpayer whenever the IRS is obtaining certain financial information.[4] These notices are required by law and are great windows into what the IRS is seeking. If a taxpayer is receiv-

---

4. I.R.C. § 7603 (2022)

ing notices for summonsed information, then you should contact the business (that is receiving the summons) and ask for a copy of the same information that is being sent to the IRS. That way, you know exactly what the IRS is receiving. Furthermore, it is generally cheaper to get copies because the IRS is paying for the research if needed. Also, contact the IRS-CI case agent and have the notices sent directly to your office. Never assume that the client is sending the notices to you in a complete and timely fashion.

Early in my IRS-CI career, the defense attorney and I were discussing various aspects of the case. He appeared to know exactly what I was seeing on the bank statements, which surprised me. He later admitted that he was getting copies of documents that I was receiving when the notices were sent to his client. When a summons notice was received by his office, he contacted that bank, and requested a copy of all documents that were sent to me. That was very smart. He knew exactly what I was reviewing.

Key Takeaway: When the IRS is required to notify you what they are seeking, get a copy of what they are receiving.

How Long Has the Case Been Open?

Ask the case agent how long the investigation has been in SCI status. SCI means Subject Criminal Investigation. With all investigations, the clock is ticking, and IRS-CI management is evaluated on the efficiency of an investigation. You won't see this in any public document, but IRS-CI evaluates the new investigations within six months to determine if they need to stay open. Around the 6-month mark, the special agent will have a discussion with their supervisor about the viability of the investigation. This is a quality control mechanism to ensure that the case is moving forward and has prosecution potential. In my opinion, the first six months is the most critical phase if you want the IRS-CI to close its investigation. It is during this time that you need to get the work done to persuade IRS-CI to stop its criminal investigation. This is a public service to IRS-CI, because if they can be persuaded to close the investigation, then they can focus their resources on other cases. Furthermore, if they can be persuaded, they really didn't have a great case to begin with. Not all cases are equal in their prosecution potential. If you don't succeed in persuading IRS-CI to close the case, then expect to wait approximately 18 months for it to be completed. You won't be offensive by selling your factual and reasonable explanation for IRS-CI to close the investigation. The worst that can happen is you hear "no."

The reason IRS-CI reviews the case in the first six months for potential prosecution is because if the special agent does not focus, he could spend two years on a case and never open a single envelope or analyze a single bank statement. IRS-CI is not in the business of having cases sit idle. It's not like wine and cheese where it gets better with age.

So, if you are representing someone in a criminal investigation, one of the questions I would ask the special agent is "how many months have elapsed on this case?" Past six months, there is more skin in the game for it to stay open. IRS-CI would rather have a marginal investigation take longer to investigate in order to have a winning prosecution, than to close a case after six months has elapsed. IRS-CI is interested in quality cases, and wants to discontinue the bad ones or marginal ones quickly, so if an agent has less than six months on it, you may have some flexibility to turn it back into a civil issue.

The average time for a completed case for IRS-CI is 18 months. Once approved by IRS management, all tax investigations go to DOJ Tax Division for final approval. The DOJ Tax Division sends the case to the United States Attorney's Office for authorizing prosecution. Then, it typically sits for a few months for an AUSA to prepare an indictment.

The bottom line is to spend money upfront for a good defense, but if it doesn't work to close the case, then expect years for it to come to the indictment stage.

Key takeaway: If an investigation is opened for less than six months (especially an administrative investigation), then gather as much information as possible to persuade IRS-CI to close its case.

File FOIA Request

File a Freedom of Information Act (FOIA) request. With a FOIA, you can receive tax information about your client, unless it impedes the investigation, such as confidential informant information, Bank Secrecy Act information, undercover agent information, etc.[5] The IRS has procedures to submit a FOIA request, which can be found on the IRS's website. FOIA requests are a pain for the agent because attorneys are now involved in gathering and evaluating the results.

Key Takeaway: A FOIA request is like a broom that sweeps up all available information that you don't currently have.

Other POAs on Account

Check for other POAs on file with the IRS. You can request this information from the case agent or your client can contact the IRS. Sometimes the client hires somebody else before or after you were hired that has the authority to negotiate with the IRS on civil matters. In one investigation I had, the defendant hired an out-of-state organization to help resolve the back taxes. Once the criminal investigation started, the defendant hired a criminal defense attorney, but that attorney had no idea that their client was speaking to the tax resolution firm, which was not covered by the attorney-client privilege. That out-of-state firm also received pertinent information from the defendant, and was never aware of the criminal tax investigation. If there are other POAs on file, then your client can revoke those POAs.

Supposedly a new POA automatically revokes the previous one, but don't assume it because section 5A of the POA allows for multiple POAs on file.

---

5. Internal Revenue Service, U.S. Dep't of Treasury, Internal Revenue Manual § 11.3.13 (2021), available at https://www.irs.gov/irm/part11/irm_1 1-003-013.

Key Takeaway: Check if other POAs are on file with the IRS and be the point of contact for your client.

Unpaid Payroll Taxes

If unpaid employment taxes are part of the criminal investigation, you may need to have a conversation with the client about possibly shutting the business down. The client needs to stop digging the hole even deeper. If the business doesn't shut down, then the business needs to start complying by making timely and accurate payroll tax deposits. It is hard for IRS-CI to justify closing an investigation if the defendant doesn't change their ways.

Key Takeaway: Particularly with unpaid payroll taxes, if the business cannot comply with its current tax obligations, then stop digging the hole deeper.

Start a Conversation with the Government

Once you have filed the POA, talk to the special agent to get a general idea of what the government is investigating. If you believe that your client has a reasonable defense or the case lacks jury appeal, make it known early in the investigation. If you are not getting a response with your reasonable excuse, talk to the supervisor or an AUSA (if there is one). Some agents don't respond as timely as you would expect.

At all times, a pleasant demeanor while talking to special agents goes a long way. In criminal tax investigations, I have found the prosecuting attorneys to be very open to a special agent's recommendations on who should be witnesses versus defendants, and which defendant should be negotiated with first. Even though special agents don't have final authority, they do have influence.

Reasonable or not, the subconscious assumption is that a defense attorney has the same attitude or disposition as their client. A prickly defense attorney is assumed to represent a prickly defendant. A highly respected criminal defense attorney told me that his reputation has to extend beyond any particular defendant. It was his ability to represent his client while maintaining a good working relationship with the prosecution team that paid dividends for his current clients and future clients. I couldn't agree with him more. I saw this firsthand when a well-respected defense attorney was retained by a defendant. That attorney came into the United States Attorney's Office, smiled and was gracious to everyone in the room. I am not a fan boy, but I experienced why he was considered one of the best. It was impressive, and at the end of the day, he was able to get his client a great outcome with the federal judge.

The best defense attorneys that I worked with listened and asked questions. I could work with those types of attorneys, which in the long run was better for their clients. I couldn't negotiate a deal, but I could determine how large the tax loss would be and if the scope of the investigation should expand into other areas. The government knows that you are representing your client. Particularly if it is an administrative investigation, your best stance is "I'm here to try to understand the problem and then fix the problem." If the case is solid against your client, then IRS-CI won't discontinue the investigation and no amount of cooperation will change the facts of the case. However, if the case is questionable or appears to be difficult, then talking their language of getting your client into compliance allows an easy exit for the agent to close the case, versus the case agent doubling down to make the investigation stick. Remember, it's compliance that IRS-CI wants.

Key Takeaway: Having a pleasant dialog pays dividends during the investigation and beyond.

Prepare Accurate Tax Returns

If you believe that a true and accurate tax return can be completed by a *Kovel* CPA, then it would be in your best interest to at least have it in your back pocket for several reasons: you will know the estimated tax loss, and the tax return can be used as part of compliance during the sentencing phase; it can also be an enticement (unsigned and unfiled of course) to show good faith for getting your client into compliance, if the administrative investigation is closed.

Be advised that a filed or amended tax return during a criminal tax investigation is considered an admission.

Early in my IRS-CI career, a defense attorney gave me an unsigned tax return as part of a potential plea agreement in the pre-indictment stage. With that return, I could recommend a tax charge that was beneficial to his client. When I notified him that it was unsigned, he stated that his client would sign it after the plea was negotiated. A signed tax return would be an admission against his client, and he didn't want to risk a false tax return violation if something was materially missing. In this case, he was using the unsigned tax return in conjunction with cooperating against another defendant. The temptation to really put the screws to his client to cooperate was now off the table. As long as the tax return appeared reasonable, I wasn't going to audit the return. I had compliance right in front of me and could use it as a basis for the plea prior to indictment. I could then move on to another case.

Key Takeaway: Hiring a professional to prepare unsigned tax returns can assist you in determining the estimated tax loss and potentially be used for compliance.

Time Factor Intent

Generally, personal tax returns are required to be filed by April 15th. If a false tax return is filed before or on that date, then that tax return can be used against the defendant. However, I learned the hard way about contacting a defendant prior to April 15th—before the tax return was filed or due. I contacted a defendant on April 13th and the defendant invoked his right to counsel. His tax return was due on April 15th, but he did not file it after that date. I was going to recommend prosecution for various tax crimes, including his failure to file for that unfiled tax year. My supervisor put a quick stop to it. She called it a "time factor intent" problem.

"How can a defendant be willful in tax evasion for that year,
if you put them on notice of an active criminal investigation?

Their defense attorney will advise them not to file a return, and you can't show willfulness when he has been advised not to file."

That was never discussed during my training in the IRS-CI academy. I should have waited a few more days for the initial interview, but I didn't know better. It could have added another count of tax evasion, particularly U.S.C. Title 26, section 7201(Spies evasion).[6] My eagerness to contact the defendant cost me a potential tax evasion count. As an example, if my initial contact with the defendant was on April 13th, 2020, then his 2019 personal tax return was due two days later. The 2019 tax year was off the table as a possible count if he failed to file afterwards.

If 1) a defendant has not filed a tax return that will be due, and 2) a special agent contacts the defendant advising them of a criminal investigation before April 15th or the extension date of October 15th, then that tax year is a freebie. Not filing on time is a misdemeanor in violation of U.S.C. Title 26, section 7203.[7] By policy, unwritten or written, IRS-CI does not recommend a failure to file violation during the year that the defendant was told that they were under investigation.

I have heard a few DOJ Tax Division trial attorneys and IRS legal counsel bemoan that defendants were told by their legal counsel to not file a tax return after being put on notice of a criminal investigation. It is still a criminal violation to not file, but defense attorneys will make the argument that their client won't file that year's tax return so as not to put their client in further jeopardy by possibly filing a false tax return. I am not an expert in legal ethics as it applies this strategy, but I do know that CPA ethics disallow advising a client not to file a timely return. As a former IRS-CI employee, I tell criminal tax defense attorneys about the "time factor intent" problem because it does reduce the number of years of possible counts and potential tax loss. But if a poison has to be picked, a

---

6. Spies v. United States, 317 U.S. 492 (1943)

7. I.R.C. § 7203 (2022)

misdemeanor for section 7203 is always better than a felony for filing a false tax return. If your client is close to the April 15th filing deadline, file the extension.

Key Takeaway: The Time Factor Intent problem can be useful if the defendant is put on notice about a criminal investigation prior to the tax return being filed.

Criminal Tax Attorneys Only

This is a pet peeve of mine. If you're not a criminal tax attorney, and you know it's a criminal tax investigation, transfer the case to a criminal tax attorney, because a non-criminal tax attorney will lose credibility quickly. Special agents know that a civil tax attorney is not attending federal court at the indictment and sentencing stages. The special agent is wasting his time dealing with non-criminal attorneys. Some defendants receive bad representation because the civil attorney wastes precious time getting any potential defenses known within six months, and also does not take advantage of any potential deals in cooperating against a conspiracy. If there's a conspiracy among four or five people, the civil attorney and incompetent criminal attorneys are always waiting until indictment and then their client is last in line for any potential plea deals. At that point there is no deal to give.

I experienced defendants hiring immigration lawyers, civil tax attorneys, traffic ticket attorneys, and even attorneys not admitted to the federal bar. It never ended well. When the indictment came, those attorneys were nowhere to be found, and another attorney had to take over.

Key Takeaway: If a criminal tax investigation is ongoing, recommend it to an experienced criminal tax defense attorney.

Don't Wait if You Have a Good Excuse

During an administrative investigation, the Power of Attorney for the defendant will be notified during certain phases of review. If you believe that you have a good defense or excuse for your client, don't wait until the final prosecution recommendation is submitted to the IRS Criminal Tax Counsel or the IRS

Special Agent in Charge (SAC). Every three or four months, a special agent updates their supervisor about their investigations. If it's an administrative case, the Power of Attorney for the taxpayer will be notified when the investigation is reviewed by the SAC for final approval. If you're waiting for that moment to attend a meeting with the SAC or Criminal Tax Counsel in order to make your argument, you've waited too long because they are aware of the pros and cons of the investigation. They have skin in the game, so by the time 18 months comes along, and you are presenting your case based on a "pretty please" or flimsy excuses, it is not going to work. I have never seen an administrative case get discontinued at the SAC level. It may have happened, but I have never heard even a story about it.

You have a better chance meeting with DOJ Tax Division when it is assigned to them for review, because they have no skin in the game. They look at it from a prosecutor's point of view. I have no history with DOJ Tax Division changing their mind on a prosecution recommendation. I know it has happened though.

Key Takeaway: If you have a good excuse, don't wait until it is too late. Your excuse fades as IRS-CI spends more time on the investigation.

Wait for Final Determination

The client needs to know to limit or stop contact with key witnesses. I have seen defendants talk to co-conspirators which later revoked their points for cooperation with the Department of Justice. With 18 months being the average time for IRS-CI to finalize its investigation, many more months will pass for DOJ Tax Division to review it and the US Attorney's Office to indict it. If, for some reason, you just don't have a very good defense, the best thing is to just let it ride to its natural conclusion. A conversation with the special agent such as, "My client is not going to be interviewed. We are looking at this investigation as well. Let me know if you come across anything that you think needs my attention," can go a long way. Let IRS-CI prove beyond reasonable doubt the criminal tax violations, but once tax violations are in an indictment, there is a 90% conviction rate.

Key Takeaway: If IRS-CI has a good case against your client, then advise your client to "do no harm" and keep their distance from key witnesses.

Chapter 9

Five Common Reasons a Case is Discontinued

T here are times that a criminal tax investigation needs to be closed. It could be one problem or a combination of problems that lead to its closure. To close an investigation, the special agent writes a closing memo detailing the allegations, the investigative steps taken, the results of the investigation, and why the case is recommended to be closed. After that memo is created, it is sent to upper management for approval. When a case is discontinued, it is called a DISCO in IRS-CI lingo.

Tax Loss

This is the most common reason an investigation is closed. Because tax loss drives the sentencing guidelines, the tax loss amount should meet the requirements at sentencing for an active prison time. Unless there are special circumstances, the tax loss will be a major factor in closing an investigation. Not meeting LEM is easiest reason to close an investigation. If the evidence doesn't prove a substantial tax loss, IRS-CI will have no problem closing its case.

Inability to Establish Responsibility

After conducting interviews, the special agent may have problems establishing responsibility. If that happens, then IRS-CI cannot overcome a reasonable reliance defense. I had cases where I didn't know who gave what document to the return preparer because the defendant had an intermediary, such as a secretary or girlfriend, who was delivering the documents to the return preparer. Not all the information was turned over to the return preparer so I could not firmly prove that the documents were in the hands of the intermediary beforehand. Or, I could not identify who prepared the books and records that had the false entries.

The other reliance defense is when the return preparer is incompetent and either does not prepare the tax return properly or does not ask the proper follow-up questions that a normal return preparer would ask. Typical follow-up questions include:

- Do you have any foreign bank accounts?

- Do these documents have all the business income for the year?

Other times, they don't review the tax return with the client prior to the client filing the tax return. A defendant's lack of tax knowledge and education coupled with an incompetent return preparer is hard for a prosecution to overcome.

Not Worth the Effort

I call this "picking up pennies to prove dollars." As I have discussed before, *Greenberg* is the major obstacle that all special agents have to overcome in a tax evasion investigation. This comes into play when the commingling of business and personal expenses have to be separated. The default position for the government is to allow the deduction. The amount of effort expended on an investigation should be correlated to a viable prosecution. There are tax investigations that cause problems because of the low amounts of transactions that are at play.

This is typical when a self-employed person commingles personal and business expenditures. Because of *Greenberg*, the special agent has to determine what expenditures are worth focusing on ($250 or over?). Early in my career, I knew a special agent who was scrutinizing small amounts (less than $100), much to the disdain of her management after three months lapsed.

If a small business owner goes out to eat and travels, the government has to prove beyond a reasonable doubt that it was a personal expense versus a business expense. If these amounts are low, like always buying lunch at Chick-fil-a, or eating occasionally at a steak house, the agent is "picking up pennies" instead of dollars. It is easier to investigate large amounts of money being disbursed that have the appearance of personal living expenses, such as private college tuition, fancy artwork, remodeling the personal residence, expensive cars driven by family members, veterinarian and grooming bills for the family dogs, etc. But if the defendant is spending low amounts of money without the large expenditures, then the special agent has to find many witnesses at low amounts, which can suck up a lot of time, and may not meet LEM.

Too Complicated for Agent

Not all special agents have the same skill set. Just because they pass the academy and are issued a gun and badge doesn't make them competent to handle all tax investigations. It is sad, but true. If a supervisor receives a new case to assign, they have to take into consideration the complexity of the case when assigning it to a special agent. Some cases are easy. Others require more specialized knowledge about a subject matter or require a special agent who can lead an investigation that involves multiple entities, co-conspirators, and bank accounts. I have seen one or two investigations be closed because of under-performing agents who cannot rise to the occasion. All too often, IRS-CI will try to work with an agent that is struggling, but if that agent doesn't have other cases to work on that are within their skill set, the supervisor allows more time to the agent to see if they can pull it off. Rarely does it end well. Upper management tries to maintain a diverse inventory of tax investigations and understands that not all special agents are created equal. If an under-performing special agent has an investigation, however simple it is, upper management will be happy to get a completed case out of them every few years.

Non-Taxable Sources of Income

This reason is usually associated with cash intensive businesses or those taxpayers who refinance their personal residence during a rising real estate market and then use the proceeds for personal living expenses. In cash intensive businesses, a cash hoard defense can take the wind out of an agent's sails real quick. An example of the cash hoard defense would be mowing grass as a teenager for years and keeping all that cash in a shoe box, only later to use it to purchase large ticket items. When cash is deposited into bank accounts or if the cash can be traced to large purchases (such as vehicles), the agent has to establish that the funds did not come from a hoard of cash kept in a shoe box for a long period of time. A smart special agent will notice that this could be a possible defense early in the investigation, and will ask questions about cash on hand for various tax years during the initial interview with the defendant.

As a special agent, every defendant that I interviewed always minimized their cash on hand when asked, believing that they would get in trouble with large amounts of cash. To negate this, I would ask if the cash would be consistent if they could not conveniently remember the exact amount each year. They would always respond "yes," which made my life easier. I then would ask if the cash was $100, $1,000, $10,000 or $100,000. They would always estimate on the low side such as $1,000. The larger the cash amount at the beginning of the investigative years, the harder the case for the special agent. Some ways that an agent can negate this defense is through bankruptcy records showing that the defendant did not claim the cash during the bankruptcy proceedings. I have also supplemented my evidence with credit applications that don't report cash on hand, but many times, the cash on hand category on that application is not the best evidence.

I was a case agent on a large illegal gambling case that involved solely cash proceeds. One concern I had was the possibility of a cash hoard defense. During the search warrant pre-operational meeting, instructions were given to agents to take good pictures and to contact me when large amounts of cash were found. When large amounts of cash were discovered in the back of the defendant's vehicle, an agent immediately took possession of the cash and made a beeline to the local bank to turn the cash into a cashier's check. The agent made no effort to take substantial pictures of the cash nor to contact me first. I was not informed of this cash discovery until after the search warrant was executed. Needless to say I was not happy. Pictures of the cash would have been at least some evidence that the cash was not from his grass mowing side hustle as a teenager.

Chapter 10

What to Do if Case is Discontinued

If your client had the good fortune to have the case discontinued, there are a few steps that can be completed to get your client into compliance, so they won't be in the same position later in life. Once the closing is confirmed, my recommendation is to hire a tax resolution expert to analyze the client's next steps. In many cases, the client needs to amend the tax returns that were being investigated by IRS-CI. The tax returns should be filed in the normal course of business. Don't bother contacting the special agent to file the amended tax returns.

Administrative

When IRS-CI discontinues an administrative criminal tax investigation, a letter will be sent to the taxpayer stating that the investigation was discontinued. This letter does not absolve the taxpayer or prevent the case from being opened again for another criminal investigation. I have learned from experience that once an administrative case is closed, the special agent moves on to other things and doesn't open the case later. With this letter bringing good news, the taxpayer can breathe a sigh of relief because they have dodged a bullet. This is a great time for the taxpayer to get into compliance with the IRS and to change their ways. IRS-CI will turn over the case file to the civil side for an audit or collection activity. IRS-CI will release its freeze on the taxpayer's account. So, the taxpayer is no longer under the threat of prison time, but they still can be harassed civilly with penalties, interest, and aggressive collection techniques.

I would recommend (if you are on good terms with the special agent) to get in touch with the special agent to obtain any financial documents that could be available to assist your client in getting into compliance. The special agent probably has bank statements, spreadsheets, copies of tax returns, etc. in their case file. This would be a great treasure trove of information, especially if the client has limited financial resources to hire professional help. The special agent is holding much of the information needed to get your client into compliance. As an authorized representative, you will have a right to these documents. In my special agent career, I never received this type of request from an attorney after a DISCO. If I did, I would know that the attorney was trying to get their client into compliance and understood the IRS mission. That would bode well in the future if the same attorney represented another defendant. Remember, compliance is what IRS-CI wants. If you ask kindly, explaining that your purpose is to get your client into compliance, you probably won't get pushback getting financial documents. Don't bother asking for copies of memorandums of interviews. Those memos have social security numbers, dates of birth, and other personal information that doesn't need to be in the hands of your client.

If a return preparer is later hired to complete a tax return or to amend an existing tax return, that return preparer does not have privileged communications in a criminal tax investigation. This may come into play if you hired a *Kovel* accountant to assist you in the criminal tax investigation. If that same accountant under a *Kovel* agreement becomes the return preparer, then privileged communications are at risk.[1]

---

1. Evan Davis, Maintaining Privileges When Kovel Accountants Prepare Tax Returns, Tax Controversy and Litig. Rep. (Tax Notes, Falls Church, VA), Oct. 1, 2018.

Grand Jury

Grand jury investigations are quite different when it comes to disclosing financial information to the civil side of the IRS. IRS-CI does not send letters to taxpayers notifying them that the grand jury investigation is closed. Any document or testimony gathered in the grand jury process cannot be turned over to the IRS civil side and is property of the grand jury. Regardless, the importance of compliance cannot be stressed enough, so hire tax professionals to get your client into compliance.

In the pre-indictment stage, there are a few types of tax cases that are unique and deserve special attention: return preparers and payroll taxes. In the next chapter, I am going to discuss the items peculiar to criminal investigations of tax return preparers.

Chapter 11

Return Preparer Investigations

Return preparer investigations are also called RPP (Return Preparer Program) investigations in IRS lingo. These investigations are on return preparers, particularly offices that prepare false tax returns on a large scale. In some neighborhoods, these rogue return preparers abuse the tax laws to get their clients large false refunds, for which the return preparers typically require a large fee.

These types of investigations are so prevalent, that a special agent can conduct these investigations during their whole career.

Here is how it typically starts:

A taxpayer gets upset and comes into the IRS office to complain about not receiving what was promised (a large refund). The taxpayer meets with IRS-CI about the missing large refund. When the special agent reviews the witness's filed tax return in the IRS computer system, false material items will be on the return, such as a false business, false education expenses, false dependents, or false income. Many times, the return preparer will add on the tax return a request for a split of the direct deposit so that the return preparer gets part of the large refund. Because the rogue return preparer wanted to hide their actions, the taxpayer will not receive a copy of the tax return. The IRS never issues the large refund either because the tax return was suspicious or the taxpayer owed an outstanding balance to the government.

Another source of RPP investigations is data mining by the IRS. During my career, the IRS had a data mining tool called RPAT (Return Preparer Analysis Tool), which wasn't widely known, but was available if an agent knew about its existence. The tool would allow special agents to analyze tax returns prepared by return preparers and return preparation businesses for anomalies and suspicious activities.

Either way, the special agent will analyze the other suspicious tax returns filed by that tax preparation business to determine if a pattern of false items develops. With that information, the special agent will wait until tax season to conduct an undercover operation on the tax preparation business. A trained undercover agent will enter the premises and request a completed tax return. The undercover agent will, of course, be recording video and audio of the exchange. Almost always there is a false tax return prepared. It is the luck of the draw who prepares the false tax return in front of the undercover agent. If there are multiple return preparers, the unfortunate one gets caught in the undercover operation. With that evidence, the special agent will request a search warrant for the premises, based on the data mining analysis and undercover operation. During the search warrant execution, the records will be seized as evidence and the team of special agents will attempt to interview as many return preparers as possible. Hopefully, one return preparer will help bust the conspiracy in the tax preparation office.

I say "hopefully" because, while these cases are not complicated in the execution of the tax scheme, they can be complicated because many return preparers are involved. Prosecuting the manager or owner of the business is a matter of getting physical evidence and getting the lower tier of return preparers to cooperate in the investigation. Rarely is there a direct link between the fraud committed by the lower level of return preparers and the management or ownership of the business. If that direct link does not exist, IRS-CI will focus on the owner's and manager's personal tax returns for any false material items.

Here are some of the common problems in an RPP investigation:

Sharing PTINs

Return preparers shops have an Electronic Filing Identification Number (EFIN) that identifies the business with the IRS. The return preparer also has a unique number called a PTIN (Preparer Tax Identification Number). This number is used by the paid return preparer and is submitted with the tax return to the IRS. It is not uncommon for PTINs to be unlawfully shared in the office. I have come across this many times: the data shows that a return preparer is preparing many false tax returns, but that PTIN was later discovered to be shared with the whole office. The PTIN owner is unaware that this identification is being used by others. The best way to prove a PTIN was stolen is to interview the taxpayers to determine who prepared the tax return. Another way is to determine if the PTIN owner was working the day the return was prepared or was employed during the time in question.

Undercover Operations

Undercover operations for RPP investigations have a twofold purpose: to obtain evidence against a bad return preparer and to get probable cause for a search warrant. IRS-CI does a good job in their undercover operations to ensure that entrapment is not a viable defense. The recorded video and audio is available during discovery, but the recording usually doesn't identify the leadership's role in the scheme.

Shady Witnesses (Shop for Large Refunds)

The witnesses in RPP investigations usually have criminal histories, sporadic job history, basic education, and are transient. A special agent usually has a team of agents to assist in the investigation, because finding these witnesses during business hours is more difficult than in a typical tax case. With these witnesses having sporadic job history and moving often, special agents spend many hours trying to find them. In addition, depending on the clientèle, they may have an aversion to law enforcement. Getting these witnesses to trial is another matter, because of lack of transportation to the courthouse and lack of child care options.

Larger Conspiracies

The nature of RPP investigations involves many return preparers. Once a scheme is taught and proven to work, the rogue return preparers will continue the same scheme. It becomes second nature for them to prepare false tax returns, and the sharing of the scheme is throughout the office. In my experience, the first return preparer to admit the scheme to law enforcement gets the better deal. In the pre-indictment stage of an investigation, a return preparer is better off cooperating with law enforcement. The larger the conspiracy, the harder it is for the co-conspirators to remain silent about their involvement. When the conspiracy falls, it falls quickly. The best attorneys get a deal quickly for their client.

Turnover of Employees

Turnover of employees is also common in the tax preparation business. In an RPP investigation, the scheme is a few years old by the time it is caught, and employee turnover is prevalent. Rarely are the same employees present each year. In most cases, once a return preparer understands the scheme and sees the potential for easy money, they will leave that office and start their own tax preparation office nearby. It is a version of the "whack-a-mole" game at the county fair. An experienced special agent who has conducted a few RPP investigations in the same area can show a link between two separate offices because one employee decided to leave and start their own business.

With the turnover of employees, it is not uncommon for the remaining employees to use the name of a former employee to hide their involvement in the scheme.

Uneducated Employees

In RPP investigations, the employees typically do not have professional certifications. The employees may have high school diplomas or are attending college while they are preparing false tax returns. The employees receive some training to prepare tax returns and to use the software, but have only a very basic knowledge of tax law. Instead of teaching the law, the "trainers" will give the employees "cheat sheets" with answers to the questions that should be asked of the taxpayer. Instead of asking the questions from the IRS form as required, the return preparer will complete the questionnaire using the cheat sheet to qualify their client for the larger refund. Furthermore, if a refund needs to be larger, the return preparer will start creating false numbers to see how it affects the refund. It is not uncommon for the return preparer in this situation to ask for advice from a more knowledgeable employee on getting a larger false tax refund. In almost every search warrant on a tax preparation business, I have found the cheat sheet.

Civil Actions Against Witnesses

When a tax return is flagged by the IRS for audit, the witness receives a notice that a potential problem exists on the return. The witness may or may not know about a false material item that shouldn't be on the tax return. Civilly, the IRS will assess an additional tax to the witness, including penalties and interest. The witness will ignore the notices, and in the subsequent year the IRS will apply the expected current refund to the prior tax bill. It is a constant cycle of IRS trying to collect on false tax returns. IRS-CI will get involved once the scheme is large enough to warrant an investigation, which is usually years down the road. When a witness owes taxes from a false tax return that was found during a civil audit, the IRS will attempt to collect payment through its collection powers. Meaning, the witness is on the hook for the false tax return from a civil perspective, but not liable criminally. This causes a headache during restitution because the special agent has to determine what exactly is owed, because some payments may already have been made between the time of the scheme and the sentencing phase.

Following the Information Flow

Rarely are the lower-level return preparers allowed to submit the tax returns to the IRS electronically. The return preparers meet their client, prepare the false tax return, and give the false tax return to a manager for final approval. The manager will then submit returns to the IRS. A question arises as to when the false material item was placed on the tax return. Was it at the return preparer level or at the manager level? When I was a special agent, my best evidence came from asking the witness for the expected refund amount. If they knew the amount, then more than likely the false material items were created at the return preparer level. In an undercover operation, a good undercover agent will ask what the expected refund is before the return is transferred from the return preparer to the manager for filing. In some cases, a receptionist enters some data on a tax return, gives the semi-finished return to the return preparer, and then the return preparer gives the return to the manager for final submission to the IRS. In that case, there are three people who could have entered the false material items that generated the larger tax refund.

Split Deposits

Split deposits are allowed on a federal tax return. The IRS should be monitoring for multiple tax refunds being deposited into the same account, but I have my doubts about some of the internal controls that the IRS puts in place to fight against tax fraud. Split deposits are common when the return preparer is receiving part of the tax refund into his or her bank account. A return preparer getting paid through a split deposit is against the IRS rules and regulations, which subjects the preparer to a penalty.[1] Split deposits show financial incentive and identify the possible bad return preparer.

Information Not in Taxpayer's File

If a search warrant is executed, the taxpayer's file should be available at the tax preparation office. A common technique is for the IRS special agent to compare the taxpayer's file found at the return preparation office to the actual tax return. Most likely, the false material item that is on the tax return is missing from the taxpayer's file. In some cases, the return preparer will tell the taxpayer what documentation needs to be provided to get a large tax refund. The return preparer will coach the taxpayer into what false documentation is needed, so that the return preparer has some type of documentation in case there is a question civilly or criminally about the contents of the tax return.

Now you know about the first unique investigation: the RPP investigation. The second type of unique investigation is the employment tax investigation.

---

1. 31 C.F.R. § 10.31 (2022)

Chapter 12

Employment Tax Investigations

A nother nuance in criminal tax investigations involves employment tax investigations. It is not uncommon for these investigations to reach millions of dollars in tax losses, because these amounts are a high percentage of gross wages and are directly related to the number of employees affected.

Employment tax investigations are based on U.S.C. Title 26, section 7202.[1]

Elements of section 7202:

1. Duty to collect, account for, and pay over a tax;

2. Failure to collect, truthfully account for, or pay over the tax; and

3. Willfulness.

In the pre-indictment stage, employment tax investigations rely on three major items: Trust Fund taxes were due, the defendant was responsible to pay them over, and the defendant didn't do it over a period of time. Like any other tax violation, the government wants a pattern of behavior, like years of time. But in employment tax investigations, the required forms are due quarterly, so there

---

1. I.R.C. § 7202 (2022)

can be four counts per year, eight counts in two years, and so on. It doesn't take long in a calendar year to show a pattern of willfulness.

There are a few considerations:

Who is the Person with this Duty?

Duty in the criminal statute goes to the definition of a "responsible party."[2] Defining a responsible party is a determination of what function the defendant plays in the collection and payment of the trust fund taxes. It is irrespective of job title. Determining the responsible party takes into consideration functions such as who is an officer of the corporation, who prioritizes expenditures, who has signature authority on bank accounts, who is signing payroll tax returns, etc. More than one person can be a responsible party. The question is: instead of paying the trust fund taxes to the government, who had the responsibility and power to divert those taxes to pay for other business expenses or personal living expenses? That in essence is how a responsible party is defined.

In most cases, the business owner will be considered a responsible party. I had one payroll tax investigation where the former business owner "sold" the business to a family member. The family member operated the business, but the former owner emotionally controlled the family member into paying for the former owner's personal living expenses instead of paying payroll taxes. Even though the former owner did not have signature authority on bank accounts and held no corporate position, she was still considered a responsible party because of her control over the funds. Both the former and current business owners were found to be responsible parties and sentenced to criminal violations of section 7202.

---

2. I.R.C. § 6672 (2022)

How Is The Tax Calculated?

In investigations into U.S.C. Title 26, section 7202, the payroll taxes (FICA tax-es and federal withholdings) that were withheld from the employees' paychecks is the tax loss. The withheld taxes are also called the "trust fund taxes." These taxes are the property of the United States that the business holds temporarily until it is to be deposited into the United States Treasury. These trust fund taxes are required to be assessed by the employer. However, if the IRS civil side needs to estimate those taxes, it can under the authority of U.S.C. Title 26, section 6020(b), which allows the IRS to create a tax return and estimate the tax liability. When the IRS estimates the tax liability using section 6020(b), it will overestimate the tax loss because it assumes a higher federal income tax withholdings rate.

Where did the Money Go?

Willfully not paying the trust fund taxes is a crime even if the funds are used to keep the business solvent, but there is no jury appeal if the funds paid business expenses. All of the 7202 investigations I have experienced involve high wages for the owner and substantial personal living expenses that were paid by the business versus paying the trust fund taxes. IRS-CI is not interested in a 7202 investigation when there is no jury appeal. Even though it could be a smaller tax loss, the 7202 charge in an indictment has a better chance of guilty verdict than other tax related charges. This type of case is easy for a jury to understand and to calculate the estimated tax loss.

For jury appeal, a special agent will spend time summarizing the disposi-tion of funds for unpaid payroll taxes that were not normal business expenses. For example, the agent will summarize the credit card payments that show disbursements to restaurants, clothing stores, gas stations, and other typical personal living expenses. *Greenberg* is not considered because the disposition is not part of the elements of the crime. A special agent will summarize where the money went, but won't opine on the business or personal nature of the expenditures. The jury will subconsciously know if the funds were for personal living expenses.

Additional Income from Trust Fund Taxes

If there is a 7202 violation being pursued, the government believes that the trust fund taxes paid for the defendant's personal living expenses. In recent years, there has been a push for adding those expenditures to the personal tax return of the defendant. So, if the trust fund taxes paid $100,000 of the defendant's personal living expenses, the government will add a count of tax evasion or filing a false tax return to the indictment. If this is done, then *Greenberg* will be in play, because the government has to prove that the defendant received personal benefit that should have been added to the defendant's personal tax return. It is a double whammy. The defendant is charged with not turning over payroll taxes in violation of 7202, but is also charged with additional counts of not reporting the personal living expenditures on the personal tax return.

Statute of Limitations for 7202 Investigations

For payroll taxes, employers are required to file a Form 941 (Employer's Quarterly Federal Tax Return). Forms 941 are calculated on a quarterly basis, but are due one month afterwards. So, since the first quarter of a year (Q1) is from January 1 to March 31, the Form 941 for Q1 is due on April 30. The Q2 payroll return is due on July 31, the Q3 payroll return is due October 31, and the Q4 payroll return is due January 31.

The statute of limitations (SOL) for filed payroll tax returns is governed by Title 26, U.S.C. section 6513(c).[3] If a payroll tax return is filed on time or a little late, the statute of limitations starts on April 15th of the next year. For example,

---

3. I.R.C. § 6513(c) (2022)

the SOL for a Q1 return filed timely on April 22 (due April 30) starts on April 15th the next year. Similarly, the SOL for a Q3 return filed late (due October 31) on December 30 starts on April 15th of the next year.

For criminal violations of 7202, the policy of the Department of Justice is that the SOL is six years, per Title 26, U.S.C. section 6531(4).[4] Though a handful of courts have found the SOL to be three years, six years is the consensus view.[5]

If the payroll tax return is filed (very late) past the April 15th date, then the SOL starts on the filed date. So, if a Q3 tax return (due October 31) is filed two years later on May 30th, then the SOL starts on the May 30th date.

If a payroll tax return is unfiled, then the SOL starts when the return was due.[6] So, if a Q3 payroll return, which is due on October 31, is unfiled, then the SOL starts on October 31. Therefore, unfiled payroll tax returns have an earlier SOL accrual date than filed payroll tax returns.

---

4. I.R.C. § 6531(4) (2022)

5. Compare United States v. Brennick, 908 F.Supp. 1004 (D. Mass. 1995), and United States v. Block, 497 F.Supp. 629 (N.D. Ga. 1980), with United States v. Gollapudi, 130 F.3d 66, 68-71 (3rd Cir. 1997), United States v. Evangelista, 122 F.3d 112, 119 (2d Cir. 1997), and United States v. Porth, 426 F.2d 519, 522 (10th Cir. 1970).

6. United States v. Phillips, 843 F.2d 438, 443 (11th Cir. 1988) (failure to file a return typically is complete on the due date of the return)

Chapter 13

Discovery

W hen the defendant has been indicted and the judicial process starts, the federal prosecutor will tell the special agent to make the case files ready for discovery. The prosecutor will request all the files pertaining to the case to be turned over. They will ask for *Brady, Jencks, Giglio*, and *Henthorn* material. For *Brady* material, special agents understand the concept. For *Jencks* material, they are not as familiar and will need some coaching from the prosecutor. My understanding is that it is prior statements by government witnesses, because they could be used for impeachment purposes on cross-examination. Not the emails that were received by the agent, for example, but the emails that were sent from his email account, and anything that the agent handwrote or typed regarding the investigation. The *Giglio* and *Henthorn* material would be directly requested by the AUSA to the case agent's management.

It is a daunting task when the prosecution sends you a CD or thumb drive with discovery material. The material isn't organized like you would prefer. Thousands of pages from hundreds of documents are common even on the smallest case. I cannot speak about other agencies and how they organize their case files or what documents should be available, but I can speak about the case files that an IRS-CI special agent should have in their possession. The question always arises as to what evidence exists in the case, what evidence was turned over during discovery, and what other information is out there that may or may not be available to be turned over during discovery.

This chapter is to help you focus on what documents you should look for and how those documents may assist you in representing your client.

Placed on a CD

As of this writing, IRS-CI can use thumb drives to download discovery, but it is rare for them to do so. IRS-CI doesn't like to use thumb drives because of the potential for viruses to spread when inserting them into government laptops. (The Department of Justice has the same concerns about inserting thumb drives into their computers, so giving thumb drives to an AUSA isn't welcomed). The most common method for discovery is to download the material onto a CD using encryption software. To combat theft of taxpayer information, IRS-CI computers require encryption when downloading files to a CD. Depending on the amount of the data, this could be on one or multiple CDs. Most of the electronic evidence will be located on the special agent's government computer, which is backed up on a regular basis to IRS-CI's server. When a case is opened, the government laptop computer creates a folder that holds the case files. As a matter of practice, I would take the case folder on the hard drive and download it to the CD, minus a few documents that are privileged. Such data would include Word, Excel, and PDF files associated with the case. Paper documents are stored in the agent's filing cabinet. If a search warrant was completed, the evidence is maintained in banker boxes. It is rare that search warrant evidence stored in banker boxes would be scanned into a PDF format. If an undercover operation occurred, those original video and audio files will be on a separate CD and most likely won't be on the agent's hard drive.

Miscellaneous Records

As mentioned, any evidence gathered from a search warrant can be expected to be in standard banker boxes. Hopefully, the records from the search warrants will be organized properly for easier retrieval.

At times, special agents use texts on their government cellphones to communicate about the case. Organizing texts related to a case was difficult. Texts on government phones are not kept separately, so the agent needs to pull those texts manually. This lack of organization also applies to emails. Emails and their attachments are the main form of communication between agents and other IRS employees. The emails are not categorized by investigation, unless the agent is well organized, so the agent will have to manually find those emails for discovery. Also in the agent's paper files are the original handwritten notes taken during an interview. Rarely are those notes scanned into PDF format.

What Won't Be in Discovery

What should not be in the discovery files are criminal histories, bank suspicious activity reports, confidential informant information, and legal opinions from IRS Criminal Tax Counsel. Experienced special agents are aware that those documents are not to be shared, but many times these files are mixed in with the other files during discovery.

What to Look for in Discovery

Here is a list of items that should be available during discovery. A checklist is available at the end of this book, or you can download the sheet at www.nord landercpa.com/discovery.

Discovery is one area that does not receive much attention in the IRS-CI training academy. It may be discussed, but never to the detail that the judicial system requires from investigators. A special agent's knowledge of discovery is very limited, so any experience in discovery is learned either from a seasoned agent or from the US Attorney's Office. From my experience with four different US Attorney's Offices, they have an open case file policy. It is better to turn over more information than not. No trial attorney wants to have discussions with judges about missing material, or information that comes late during the pre-trial process. I have received some training from the US Attorney's Office, and the bottom line is that they want everything turned over to the defense, down to the Post-It notes that were used to write various thoughts. The practicality of that request escapes me, but I understand what they were trying to convey.

Here are the top items that you should immediately inspect in discovery. When reviewing discovery, focus on the first item, which is approximately 95% of the government's tax case: the case agent's prosecution report.

Special Agent's Report (SAR)

The acronym SAR has dual meanings in the IRS-CI lexicon. It means Suspicious Activity Report, which is a product from FinCen. That SAR cannot be in discovery. It is considered privileged material not to be shared outside the law enforcement community.

The other meaning is Special Agent's Report, and is also known as a Pros Report, which is short hand for prosecution report. This SAR created by the case agent is required for criminal tax investigations. It embodies all of the pertinent information that IRS-CI, its legal counsel, and DOJ Tax Division require to prove the recommended tax crimes that should be prosecuted. More detail is listed in IRM Section 9.5.8.6.[1]

In essence, the SAR has multiple sections that help the reader understand the facts of the case and the recommendations based on those facts. This report is created by the case agent and reviewed by many others: immediate supervisor, a centralized case reviewer (CCR), IRS Criminal Tax Counsel, IRS-CI's upper management, DOJ Tax Division, and the United States Attorney's Office. Because of its preparation and organization, it is also the road map for any potential criminal tax trial. When the time comes, the report is an excellent resource for the United States Probation Office for preparing the pre-sentencing report. It is

---

1. Internal Revenue Service, U.S. Dep't of Treasury, Internal Revenue Manual § 9.5.8.6 (2015), available at https://www.irs.gov/irm/part9/irm_09 -005-008.

the most useful tool that you will find in discovery. Here are the main sections of the SAR:

Cover Sheet

Table of Contents

Body of Report

- INTRODUCTION

- Recommended Charges and Prosecution Years

- Returns Filed and Statute of Limitations

- Venue

- Investigative Contact(s) with Subject(s) and/or Representative(s)

- Other Pertinent Data

- THEORY OF THE INVESTIGATION

- BOOKS AND RECORDS AND PREPARATION OF TAX RE-TURN(S)

- ELEMENTS OF THE OFFENSE(S)

- LIST OF APPENDICES

- DISPOSITION OF PROCEEDS

- RELEVANT CONDUCT

- CURRENT LIFESTYLE / RECENT AND POST-OFFENSE FACTORS

- EXPLANATIONS AND/OR DEFENSES OF SUBJECT

- CONCLUSIONS AND RECOMMENDATIONS

List of Witnesses and Exhibits

Appendices

Summary of Witness Testimony and Records (Optional)

Exhibits

The SAR is a PDF file that is linked to all the evidence to support a prosecution recommendation. For every allegation or fact, the report will have a link that will take the user to the evidence that is embedded further down in the report. The report is a narrative and the evidence is organized by the witness who can introduce the evidence at trial. The SAR will most likely be hundreds if not thousands of pages long. As a hint, the report is very easy to use, but the instructions are at the end of the PDF file, so printing the instructions and shortcut keys to move around the report will be well worth your time. Most defense attorneys are not aware of the users manual at the end of the report.

The SAR is the narrative of the prosecution recommendation, which will include:

Recommended Charges - what charges are recommended and the tax years involved.

Venue - where the charges should be brought. Interestingly, the place of business or defendant's residence does not establish venue, except if it is a failure to file violation.

Statute of Limitations (SOL) - For each charge, the statute of limitations is reported, so that no violation is outside the SOL. For most Title 26 investigations, the SOL is six years.[2] For employment tax investigations, there are peculiar rules if the form is filed or not filed. Furthermore, two districts (Massachusetts

---

2. I.R.C. § 6531 (2022)

and Northern Georgia) have concluded that the SOL is 3 years for employment tax violations.[3]

Tax Returns Being Investigated - the tax returns that are at the center of the investigation or, if needed, proof that the returns are not in the IRS system. Also with the tax returns are the transcripts that are maintained by the IRS to prove the tax returns were processed and any other activity associated with the defendant's accounts. The transcripts are expected to be current (within 90 days of the report). Sometimes tax returns that are not part of the elements of the crime are also exhibited in this section if those tax returns are relevant to the investigation, such as if they reveal relevant conduct.

Investigative Contact with Subject - the various contacts with the defendant, including the advice of rights.

Brief Information - defendant's personal identifiers, citizenship, education, health, business history, knowledge of tax matters, criminal history, civil IRS history, search warrant activity, undercover activity, and other pertinent information

Theory of the Investigation - a summary of the investigation, which will include how the case was discovered, who the defendant is, what the defendant did, for how long, and the total expected tax loss. Also in the theory section should be a statement about the spouse's culpability, any co-conspirators, the method of accounting (which is almost always on a cash basis), and the method of proof (which is almost always a specific item method of proof).

Books and Records - In this section, the books and records are discussed, such as who maintained them, how IRS-CI got access to the records, how the records were analyzed, and a comparison of the records to the tax returns. This section also discusses the preparation of the tax returns if they are related to the books and records. The agent is also expected to show any discrepancies between the books and records and the tax returns, and how it affects the investigation, if at all.

---

3. See United States v. Brennick, 908 F.Supp. 1004 (D. Mass. 1995); United States v. Block, 497 F.Supp. 629 (N.D. Ga. 1980).

Elements of the Offense - for each count, the elements of the offense are listed, with evidence to support each element.

Disposition of Proceeds - Although not an element of any criminal tax violation, it shows intent and jury appeal. In return preparer investigations, the disposition is rarely used.

Potential Defenses - If a defendant gave a defense, this section shows what was said and any rebuttal against it.

List of Appendices - Tax investigations are spreadsheet intensive. The appendices support how the tax loss was calculated and what tax years apply. By exhibiting the witness and evidence, any potential *Greenberg* problems are solved in the appendices. The appendices are created in Excel but are printed in a PDF format. If not in discovery, request the original Excel files to verify the amounts.

Relevant Conduct - includes all information that will have an impact at sentencing. This could include tax years outside the scope of the investigation.

Current Lifestyle - a brief explanation of the defendant's lifestyle: if they have changed their ways, loss of their livelihood, etc.

Conclusion - based on the evidence in the report, how many counts and what violations are recommended.

List of Witnesses and Exhibits - a great summary of what evidence supports the allegations and who the witness will be to introduce it at trial.

Appendices - appendices proving the elements of the crime and other pertinent data. The appendices are the heart of the investigation. They show the dates, amounts, descriptions of the evidence, who the witness will be, etc. Criminal tax computations are listed in their own appendix.

Key Takeaway: All of the government's allegations of tax crimes against the defendant are exhibited in the SAR. In one PDF file, the SAR will get you 95% there in your review.

If the SAR is most of the case, what exactly should you be looking for in addition to the prosecution's version of the facts?

MFTRA -C

A MFTRA -C is a command code (Master File Transcript -Complete) that is in the IRS database called IDRS (Integrated Data Retrieval System). Every special agent knows what MFTRA -C is. It is a complete transcript of the taxpayer's account which shows the tax filing date, adjustments made to the account, if it was referred for audit or collection, letters sent to the taxpayer, and if a refund was issued or credited to another tax year. It is based on the type of tax and period, and the information is not user friendly. It will be many pages long, with "MFTRA" listed on the top. If you can read it in English, then you don't have it, because every action taken by the IRS requires a transaction code. For example, instead of printing "tax return filed" in English, the MFTRA will have "TC 150" with a date. TC 150 (Transaction Code 150) is computer language that a return was filed. Whenever a special agent refers a tax crime to the US Attorney's Office, a MFTRA is required to be attached.[4]

What is Typically on the MFTRA?

- Tax return being filed

- Substitute return filed by IRS

- Penalties and interest assessed

- Power of attorney approval

- Balance due

- Bankruptcy proceeding started

---

4. Internal Revenue Service, U.S. Dep't of Treasury, Internal Revenue Manual § 9.5.8.6.3.1.2(2) (2022), available at https://www.irs.gov/irm/part9/irm_09-005-008

- Tax payments made

- Refunds issued

- Liens filed

- Levies filed

- Collection activity

- Exam activity

- Criminal investigation started and finished

- Notices sent to taxpayer (type, date, and amount)

Deciphering the MFTRA transcript takes experience and even a veteran IRS agent will sometimes need to refer to a handbook to determine what a command code is referencing.

During my special agent career, I referenced the MFTRA -C multiple times to prove that the taxpayer was notified that his tax returns were under audit, sent to collection, demand payment, warnings of levies, etc. Whenever the IRS sends a standard notice to the taxpayer, it is recorded in the MFTRA.

The MFTRA should be exhibited in the SAR as part of the evidence mentioned earlier in this chapter.

Key Takeaway: The MFTRA -C gives a full picture of the activities of the IRS on a defendant's account.

Diary

IRS-CI keeps statistics and investigations in CIMIS (Criminal Investigations Management Information System). When an investigation is created in CIMIS, CIMIS requires the investigation to be assigned to an IRS-CI special agent. This is called an agent's "inventory." If you hear the word "inventory" this means that under the case agent's name, all of the assigned investigations are listed for which they are personally responsible. The CIMIS report will show the status of each investigation, whether the case just started, is being reviewed by others, at DOJ Tax, or at the sentencing phase.

There are various stages that an investigation is recorded in CIMIS. The agent's diary feeds the daily activity of the agent into CIMIS, which feeds into other aspects of CIMIS. Ultimately, IRS-CI uses this information to monitor the progression of the investigation, with the agent's diary entries being the basic building blocks of activity. If an agent has zero hours applied to an active investigation, management may ask the agent why they are not working on that case. Sometimes there may be a reasonable excuse, such as vacation, training, or other competing investigation priorities. The bottom line is that the diaries of agents help management know what cases are being actively worked and the diary is required to list a daily activity in the narrative portion. It is a tool ensuring that expectations are being met.

IRS-CI special agents are paid via a bi-weekly salary, based on a 50-hour workweek (10 of the 50 hours is called LEAP, which is overtime). To keep tabs on the agents and the case progression, IRS-CI requires a diary to be completed and uploaded on a monthly basis into CIMIS. This diary consists of the minimum: 1) case number, 2) case name, 3) hours worked per day, and 4) description of activity completed. Depending on the agent, the description of activity can be very few words or paragraphs. The range of detail can vary greatly, leaning more toward a few notes in the description.

Per IRM section 9.12.1.2, the diary is to be detailed for daily activity.[5] In the private sector, billing for every six minutes or a tenth of an hour is common. Special agents don't have that pressure to record their activity in tenth of an hour increment. No bill is being generated or disputed by the client, so time spent on a case isn't exactly recorded with precision. Agents are on the honor system that they are working 50-hour weeks, with the daily diary to be uploaded by the

---

5. Internal Revenue Service, U.S. Dep't of Treasury, Internal Revenue Manual § 9.12.1.2 (2008), available at https://www.irs.gov/irm/part9/irm_0 9-012-001

agent into CIMIS monthly. Agents don't punch in and out like a factory worker earning an hourly wage. IRS-CI management reviews the diary to determine if an agent is working on a case, or how many hours are being used to work on an investigation. Each investigation has its own complexity, so the number of hours spent on an investigation isn't very relevant in management's decision making. What is relevant is the elapsed number of days the case is assigned to an investigator.

Per IRM section 9.12.1.2, the following directives apply to the diary:

- Keep diaries current and up-to-date.

- Entries should be brief but detailed enough to describe the employee's activities with respect to official matters, such as investigative actions, leave, Law Enforcement Availability Pay (LEAP), overtime/credit/compensatory hours worked, travel expenses, vehicle log including home-to-work entries, official expenditures, etc.

- Entries should cover important activities, such as initial interview of taxpayers, interviews of return preparers or key witnesses.

- Entries should be of sufficient length to describe the event. This would include sources, dates of origin, and other facts and circumstances involved in obtaining leads and evidence in investigations.

- Law Enforcement Availability Pay (LEAP) entries should be specific as to the time and details of all activities.

In a criminal trial, I sent my diary as part of discovery. The defense attorney tried to use my diary against me—commenting to the jury about the number of hours that were spent on the case, as if to insinuate that I was on a vendetta against his client. Part of his questioning revolved around the number of hours that I spent on the investigation. I spent approximately 700 hours on the investigation. It isn't uncommon for an agent to spend 1,000 hours or more on an investigation. An agent probably works three active cases at a time, with an average 18 months to complete. Using basic math, a typical 2,000-hour work year divided by 3 would be a little over 600 hours per year. If you multiply 600 hours in 1.5 years or 18 months, it comes to approximately 900 hours, which is close to 1,000 hours. Again, that is average for 18 months. A more complex investigation would require more time by the case agent and, more than likely, other agents would be recording their activity in their diary as well, which is totaled for the number of hours compiled in CIMIS. This is to give you a reference for gauging an agent's time spent on the investigation as recorded in a diary.

If the case agent is working an investigation, assistance is always given by other agents. These other agents will record in their own diary the case name, case number and activity description.

What trips up agents is when their diary is inconsistent with an important activity that is mentioned elsewhere. The diary should be consistent with the other work completed by the agent.

Key Takeaway: The special agent's diary gives you a timeline of events, which may be helpful if there is a dispute about their activities to impeach them on cross-examination, but don't assume that their diaries are the same as normal professional time sheets.

Emails and Texts

Emails and texts should be available from the case agent. Documents from other agents who assisted in the investigation should be turned over as well. For the most part, agents know that their communications are open to discovery. I would expect most of the emails to be mundane scheduling requests, passing back and forth memos to review for accuracy, etc.

Key Takeaway: Emails and texts are manually filtered for discovery. Agents are aware their emails and texts are part of the discovery process.

Reconcile the Bank Accounts

In almost every financial crime, a financial institution is used to move the funds. Whether it is a deposit or expenditure, a careful analysis needs to be completed, especially in tax evasion crimes. IRS-CI special agents often break an important rule of forensic accounting, that is, you always reconcile the bank accounts to the spreadsheets. This error, in my opinion, comes from federal agents who don't have a private sector background, such as auditing, whereby bank accounts are reconciled to the financial statements as part of standard operating procedures.

Why is Reconciliation Important?

A reconciliation is important because it proves that all funds are accounted for. Just like a law firm is required to reconcile its trust fund accounts, financial crime investigators must reconcile the source documents. I have seen it missed in the following ways: A federal agent is trying to determine the source and disposition of funds. The agent will either 1) miss an important transaction or 2) input the wrong number by mistake. Instead of $2,000 entered in the agent's spreadsheet, the number becomes $20,000. Without reconciling the account, the error may be perpetuated. This becomes even more true in Excel, which is used by many federal agents. Excel does not have a built-in reconciliation function. The function has to be created by the agent within Excel. Just because a bunch of numbers are on a spreadsheet doesn't mean that the numbers are correct.

In one example, I was tasked by a supervisor to review a fellow agent's investigation to determine if the case could be salvaged. The agent wasn't moving the case along per management's expectations. The case was getting old and the agent appeared to be stuck or the case was too complex for his skillset. This is a more common occurrence than you would think. I was given the assignment to meet with the agent, gather his files, ask pertinent questions, review what had been done or should have been done, and report back my findings to the supervisor.

One of the first things I request in reviewing a financial investigation is the spreadsheet the agent created to prove the flow of money. I want to know where the money came from and where it went. This spreadsheet should be an exact reflection of the bank accounts. In this case, I discovered that the agent did not reconcile his spreadsheet to the bank statements. Upon further inspection, his spreadsheet was missing deposits that he later admitted he was unaware of, which could create a positive or negative outcome for the investigation. The bottom line is that the missing deposits on his spreadsheet were substantial enough to change the trajectory of the investigation. That mistake alone was enough to question whether the investigation could be salvaged rather than discontinued. My report to management mentioned these missing deposits as part of my evaluation of undone tasks, which didn't put the agent in a good light about the effectiveness of the investigation. If I could find mistakes easily because of the failure to reconcile the flow of funds, what else was missing from the investigation? The investigation was closed because management didn't believe that more time spent on the investigation would result in a viable prosecution.

With many agents using Excel spreadsheets (which this agent did), look or ask for some type of reconciliation to the source documents. When I was training new agents, I preached the importance of reconciling the source documents to the spreadsheets so they don't make these mistakes. I learned that if the agent doesn't have a private sector audit background, many times they don't reconcile their work, which can be embarrassing if mistakes are discovered.

Key takeaway: Ask the agent for proof of reconciliation of their spreadsheet to the source documents. Hire an expert to reconcile the agent's provided spreadsheet with the source documents, so that any errors can be found and used.

Reconcile the Books and Records to Tax Returns

Reconciliation isn't limited to bank accounts. It should also be completed for what the return preparer received and what was reported on a tax return, particularly if financial statements or documents were given to the return preparer by the defendant or defendant's representative. During an investigation, the case agent needs to compare what information was given to the return preparer to what was reported on the tax return. If there is a discrepancy, which often there is, then the case agent needs to determine if the return preparer's mistake is fatal to the criminal tax investigation. This reconciliation should be mentioned in the SAR but may not be.

Key Takeaway: The special agent should be able to show the flow of information from the defendant to the filed tax return.

6020(b) vs Reality

United States Code Title 26, section 6020(b) gives the IRS the statutory authority to prepare a tax return and assess taxes on unfiled tax returns.[6] As you can imagine, when the IRS estimates the tax liabilities, it greatly overestimates the deficiency. For example, the IRS won't know, and therefore won't take into consideration, tax deductions that could be legitimately taken by the taxpayer.

What makes it worse is when the government can assume the amount of taxes were withheld from employees' paychecks. If an employment tax return isn't filed, employee wages are estimated and the statutory federal and FICA withholdings are estimated. If federal withholdings need estimation, 20% of the gross wages are used.[7] This does not include the FICA withholdings that are required at 7.65% from the employee and the matching amounts for the employer.

Think of it this way: when an IRS agent is tasked with estimating the taxes due from unpaid payroll taxes, he can estimate from various sources of information, both inside and outside the IRS. One source is the IRS itself. When an

---

6. I.R.C. § 6020(b) (2022)

7. Internal Revenue Service, U.S. Dep't of Treasury, Internal Revenue Manual § 5.18.2.2.2.1 (2020), available at https://www.irs.gov/irm/part5/irm_05-018-002r

employee electronically files a personal income tax return, the wages from their employer are reported on the tax return, including the withholdings. By conducting a query of all the employees reporting wages from a certain employer, an agent can calculate wages and withholdings from those electronically filed tax returns. With that amount, the agent can generate a 6020B filing for the Forms 941 that should have been filed.

A second source will be from the employer itself. Code of Federal Regulations Title 26, section 31.6051-1(a)(3) requires that employers keep copies of Forms W-2 that were issued to the employees, but not delivered. If an employee cannot be located, then copies of the Forms W-2 are required to be kept for four years.[8] With most businesses, employees will harass the employer if they do not receive a Form W-2 for their yearly wages, so it is not uncommon for the business to retain those records even if the Form W-2s were never filed with the government. If the employer does not have the records but uses a payroll service, then that payroll service can turn over the records. But let's assume that the employer did not want to cooperate with the IRS, had no payroll service, and didn't want to turn over Form W-2s or maybe didn't have them because of a fire, flood, etc. What then? Most states have an unemployment insurance program that is funded by the employer. When wages are paid, a percentage of those wages are taxed and paid by the employer, and turned over to the state. In North Carolina for example, the employer is required to file quarterly statements showing the employee's social security number, name, and wages. Most states are aggressive in requiring these forms to be filed accurately and timely. When I was a CPA in public accounting, audits of wages to calculate state unemployment insurance were more common than federal audits. That being said, the IRS and the state taxing authorities typically have a memo of understanding to share information for tax enforcement purposes. Therefore in North Carolina, the IRS agent can get this information from the unemployment commission and, using its 6020B authority, recreate a Form 941 based on the wages that were reported to the state.

---

8. Treas. Reg. § 31.6051-1(a)(3) (1960)

This is the most common way to calculate employee wages when a business is not cooperating with the IRS collection activity.

I can't think of a 6020B tax calculation that would be beneficial to the defendant, unless the IRS has no knowledge about substantial unreported wages. I conducted a criminal tax investigation into employment tax fraud. The business had over 100 employees, but failed to file employment tax returns for years. A civil examination using 6020(b) authority estimated the tax liabilities to be millions of dollars, but in reality the amount due was much less. The business hired a CPA to prepare the payroll tax returns, but never filed them. During the search warrant of the business the unfiled payroll tax returns were discovered. After this discovery, I had a conversation with the defense attorney. My recommendation was for his client to file the accurate tax returns, so there is no dispute about the accuracy of the loss. It was in the defendant's favor, and made my job easier because I didn't need to prove the tax loss. It was a win-win for all of us. Furthermore, the defense could state at sentencing that the defendant learned the valuable lesson, is trying to comply, etc. to earn the good graces of the judge.

Key takeaway: U.S.C. Title 26, Section 6020(b) allows the IRS to prepare a SFR (Substitute for Return) a.k.a. 6020B calculation. This estimate grossly overstates the tax loss. See if there is a way to calculate a reasonable loss amount.

Greenberg Problem

As mentioned previously in this book, *Greenberg* is a court case that requires special agents to interview witnesses to determine whether a deduction is business or personal. IRS-CI does a good job overcoming these issues, but it is worth reviewing evidence to ensure that it is being followed.

IRM Section 9.5.1.14 states -

> [T]he government must be prepared to call third-party payees as witnesses or introduce other independent testimonial or documentary evidence to establish the purpose of the payments.

Failure to do so would create a so-called 'Greenberg problem,' named after a First Circuit case of that name.[9]

Key Takeaway: Make sure that the tax calculations are supported by the appropriate witness and evidence.

Civil Tax File

If the tax investigation started as a fraud referral, IRS-CI should have a copy of the civil agent's file. You will be surprised how many agents don't ask for it during the investigation. There is a wealth of information that will be in the civil tax file. If the investigation is not a fraud referral, but there is substantial collection activity against the defendant, a civil tax file will still exist. IRS-CI should already have the file from the civil side, but they can get their hands on the file if needed. A MFTRA -C will notify you of any civil activities.

The civil file will have paper documents, but not necessarily the ICS history. The ICS history is maintained electronically by taxpayer identification number (business and personal are separate), so you will need to request a paper copy per entity.

In reviewing many civil tax files as a special agent, I discovered that when a defendant was interviewed by the revenue officer, the revenue officer will complete a Form 433A (Collection Information Statement) as part of their standard procedures. The Form 433A is a list of assets and income that is signed under penalties of perjury by the defendant. On more than one occasion, the form is completed in the revenue officer's handwriting, and sometimes is not signed by the taxpayer. This caused me problems because it is difficult to prove beyond a reasonable doubt that the defendant was 1) asked all the pertinent questions or 2) understood all the questions if asked. Furthermore, the Form

---

9. Internal Revenue Service, U.S. Dep't of Treasury, Internal Revenue Manual § 9.5.1.14 (2011), available at https://www.irs.gov/irm/part9/irm_0 9-005-001

433A cannot be used as a potential count for filing a false tax return if it was never signed. The revenue officer took shortcuts during the interview process, and then later I could not trust the contents of the Form 433A as a complete statement by the defendant.

Per *Tweel*, as previously mentioned in this book, a criminal investigation cannot be conducted under the guise of a civil examination.[10] Furthermore, civil agents are not allowed to use deceit or trickery. Reviewing memorandums of interviews, talking to the defendant, and reviewing the civil agent's case file can point to a *Tweel* problem if it exists.

Key Takeaway: Review the civil tax file for potential errors made by the civil agent, such as unsigned returns, returns completed in the revenue officer's handwriting, etc. Although rare, look at the evidence for any Tweel *violations.*

Search Warrant Results

If a search was conducted of the defendant's premises or of their computer, then evidence from the search warrant results directly related to the elements of the crime should be in the SAR. However, search warrants are typically paper intensive, therefore, evidence of the search warrant should be in boxes along with sketches, entry photos/videos, and exit photos/videos. Because digital evidence is found on computers and phones, IRS-CI most likely assigned a computer forensic expert to download the information from the defendant's electronics. If that happened, you may need to hire a computer expert to review the digital documents retrieved during the search warrant. IRS-CI uses specialized forensic software to review electronically stored evidence. This software doesn't allow you to review documents on your own computer. There may need to be a request for your own computer forensic examiner to review the files or request the results to be on a virtual computer, so you can access the data yourself. If you desire to get a copy of seized electronic files, bring a blank external hard drive to

---

10. United States v. Tweel, 550 F. 2d 297 (5th Cir. 1977)

IRS-CI's forensic examiner. IRS-CI doesn't keep blank hard drives available to load evidence for defense counsel.

For electronic information, the computer forensic expert downloads and verifies the files found on the electronic device. In the forensic process, a computer examiner will review the evidence for anything of value to the investigation, make a list of files found, and notify the case agent. I was never a fan of this policy because I knew more about the investigation than anyone else and I didn't want someone else to filter potential evidence for me. My guess would be that IRS-CI doesn't want compromising photos of the defendants or witnesses to be given to the case agent.

I remember one case where I needed all texts and photos on the defendant's cell phone. It was hard trying to get all the raw information, but I succeeded. True to form, the defendant received photos and sent photos that were adult oriented. However, these photos were helpful in identifying girlfriends for the disposition of proceeds. Furthermore, the texts, along with the photos, showed a more intimate relationship than what was previously stated by the defendant.

All this being said, IRS-CI special agents may not be privy to all information stored on an electronic device because it was filtered by the computer forensic examiner.

Search Warrant Evidence Chain Of Custody

If there is a weakness in IRS-CI financial investigations, it would be in preserving the chain of custody of paper search warrant material. IRS-CI is great at finding and evaluating information. There is plenty of training at the IRS-CI academy on how to conduct a thorough search.

Typically here is what happens during a search warrant execution: the special agents will secure the premises first. After the premises are secured, a designated agent will photograph or video-record the premises to show the condition of the location prior to the agents searching for evidence. These are called "entry photos." A different agent will sketch the layout of the premises and label rooms to show where any evidence was located. Agents will then start their search in a systematic manner, pairing up in rooms. If evidence is found, they will "bag and tag" the evidence, initial the label on the evidence bag, and give the evidence to the evidence custodian. The custodian will input the label information into a database so that there is a record of seized evidence. After the search is completed, the custodian will print an inventory listing items that were seized pursuant to Rule 41 of the Federal Rules of Criminal Procedure.[11] A designated agent will take "exit photos" or videos to show how IRS-CI left the premises. The boxes of evidence will be carried to an agent's vehicle and then stored in IRS-CI's office.

IRS-CI stores evidence in an evidence room that is protected with a manual cipher lock. All special agents and support staff in that office have access to the evidence room. When an agent decides to look through the boxes of evidence in a more detailed fashion, the agent will take the box(es) out of the room to a conference room or his or her cubicle and start the review. The evidence bags will be opened and analyzed, with the documents placed back into the bag. There is not an evidence custodian like you would see in local police departments where the chain of custody is known each time an item is removed or stored. In IRS-CI's method of operation, the agent walks in, gets the box, reviews the evidence, puts it back in its original container, delivers it back to the evidence room and shuts off the light when they leave. They don't have a systematic logbook like a local police department.

This current system is inconsistent with the third paragraph in IRM section 9.4.9.3.6.1, which requires a log for each activity.[12] I have never seen a log book completed by an agent. I don't think most of them even know about its required existence. Nor have I heard of a defense attorney scrutinize the lack of an evidence log book. Being a non-attorney, I can only imagine the possible problems.

---

11. Fed. R. Crim. P. 41

12. Internal Revenue Service, U.S. Dep't of Treasury, Internal Revenue Manual § 9.4.9.3.6.1 (2005), available at https://www.irs.gov/irm/part9/irm_09-004-009

Here is the third paragraph of IRM section 9.4.9.3.6.1 (02-09-2005) for preserving the chain of custody:

"The Evidence Access Control Log form is designed to record and document all access to controlled areas where evidence is stored. The form is formatted to record access to the storage location or a specific evidence storage container such as a wire cage, file cabinet, envelope, box, etc. The official evidence custodian is required to record an access entry no more than one time per day. Everyone else is required to record an access entry for each and every instance when they enter the controlled access area. The "notes" section for each access entry, except those for the official evidence custodian, is used to record specific information about the purpose for entering the controlled access area, identify what evidence was accessed, and specify the reason for accessing the evidence. The form is kept with the evidence at the secured storage location."

Key Takeaway: For search warrant evidence, paper evidence will be stored in banker boxes in the evidence room. Electronic evidence will be stored and analyzed by a computer forensic examiner. For paper documents, there should be a logbook when storing and receiving evidence. If you want to review electronic evidence, bring a portable hard drive. Reviewing paper evidence will most likely be completed at IRS-CI's offices.

Undercover Operations

If there is an undercover operation, there will be memos detailing who was present, date, time, and a summary of events. There will also be a separate memo from the undercover agent about what they saw and heard. An undercover agent will have an audio and video recording device with them during the meeting.

After the undercover operation, a tech agent (who specializes in covert record-ings) will retrieve the recording device from the undercover agent. The recording device will be downloaded to the tech agent's computer. This computer is for tech agents only, so it is separate from a special agent's computer. The tech agent will make multiple copies of the recorded video and audio files for the case agent and seal the original recording in an evidence envelope. The case agent will then use the working copies during the investigation. Sometimes a transcription service will be hired to transcribe the audio of the meeting.

In return preparer cases, IRS-CI will use the undercover operations to estab-lish probable cause that the return preparation business is engaging in criminal tax violations. The undercover operation may engage with one or more return preparers, depending on the situation, availability of undercover agents, and financial resources available for such operations. So, don't be surprised if your defendant was not the target of the undercover operation. Many times, it is the luck of the draw of who is the available return preparer that is ultimately recorded.

Key Takeaway: If there is an undercover operation, there should be memos from the undercover agent and an audio and video copy on a separate CD from the discovery CD.

Agent's Notes

Special agents are trained very well in how to conduct financial interviews and the importance of taking copious notes during such interviews. Most interviews have two agents present, with one agent asking questions while the other agent is taking notes. The interviewing agent should also take notes, but those will be limited because the agent has to listen, think, write, and ask good follow-up questions. When an agent conducts an interview, there should be handwritten notes from the interviewing agent and the secondary agent. These notes from both agents are maintained in the case agent's files. Every agent has their own process for storing these notes. During my career, I stored the handwritten notes from both agents in the witness folder, maintained in my filing cabinet.

Interview notes are rarely scanned into an electronic file, so if you want to review the special agent notes, those notes are probably in the agent's filing cabinet, and not on a discovery disk.

The notes from both agents are used to create a MOI (Memorandum of Interview). MOIs are part of IRS-CI's lexicon. The MOIs are the basic building blocks for recording the conversation between the agent and the interviewee. Special agents know not to destroy those notes. Per the IRM 9.4.5.7.4 , the MOI is to be created within a reasonable period of time.[13] There is no formal oversight on the timeliness of writing MOIs. The onus is on the agent to write the memo timely.

Key Takeaway: The special agents should have handwritten notes to accompany the MOIs, but most likely those notes are stored in the agent's filing cabinet.

Tax Return Filed by Spouse?

If a defendant has failed to file tax returns, many special agents won't research the spouse's filing status. Sometimes a defendant's lifestyle comes from the spouse or boyfriend/girlfriend. This can be an Achilles heel for the prosecution, because the spouse or live-in may have reported some income that was associated with the defendant, or the spouse could have been the responsible party for reporting the income. It depends on the situation, but if your defendant is married, check for any tax returns filed by the spouse. The case agent may or may not have this information. I have heard of one case (not mine) in which IRS Criminal Tax Counsel requested the spouse's tax returns during their review of the prosecution report, only to discover that the income was on the spouse's return unbeknown to the case agent, leaving the investigation with a potential fatal error to overcome.

---

13. Internal Revenue Service, U.S. Dep't of Treasury, Internal Revenue Manual § 9.4.5.7.4 (2008), available at https://www.irs.gov/irm/part9/irm_0 9-004-005

Key Takeaway: If necessary, inquire about the tax returns of the spouse or live-in boyfriend/girlfriend to see if they reported any income that could support the defendant's lifestyle.

Statute of Limitations Confusion

In the SAR, the statute of limitations is explicitly mentioned, so there should be no confusion about the first day a violation is barred from prosecution. Generally, Title 26 violations have a six-year statute of limitations.[14] For tax evasion, the last date of the affirmative act is when the clock starts. For filing a false tax return, the clock starts when the return is filed or when it is due, whichever is later. I have seen many defense attorneys get animated thinking that the statute of limitations is five years when the government cuts it close on the indictment date. There are some weird rules about tax violations regarding payroll tax returns, which I discussed in the employment tax section in this chapter. Because the payroll tax forms are due every quarter, each quarter stands by itself.

- I.R.C § 7201 (tax evasion) - Six years after the last affirmative act of evasion

- I.R.C § 7203 (failure to file) - Six years after the tax return was due.

- I.R.C. § 7206(1) and (2) (filing a false tax return) - Six years after the tax return was filed or due, whichever is later.

- I.R.C. § 7202 (unpaid payroll taxes) - Six years after April 15th of the next year or when filed, whichever is later. If failed to file, six years after the return was due. This was already discussed in a previous chapter.

Key Takeaway: Check the statute of limitations on the tax violations, particularly for the employment tax violations.

---

14. I.R.C. § 6531 (2022)

Social Security Administration for Form W-2s

In most section 7202 investigations, the payroll tax returns (such as Forms 941) are not filed, the tax deposits are not paid, and Form W-2s are not filed properly. If the quarterly payroll tax returns are not filed, it usually goes hand-in-hand that the yearly Forms W-2 reporting employee wages are not filed with the government. Contrary to the public's misunderstanding, the employer is required to file the Form W-2s with the Social Security Administration (SSA), not the IRS.[15] This misunderstanding commonly creeps into the indictment, whereby the indictment assumes that the IRS receives the Form W-2. Behind the scenes, when the SSA receives a copy of the Form W-2 from the employer, the SSA shares it with the IRS, so the IRS records showing W-2 employment are really a copy of the SSA file.

If the indictment tells the story of the missing Form W-2s, the Social Security Administration should be in the indictment as the proper recipient of the Form W-2. I caught this often reviewing the draft indictment before the grand jury received it. So, during trial, proof that the W-2s were not filed should come directly from the Social Security Administration, not the IRS.

Key Takeaway: Review the indictment for references to missing Form W-2s that should be filed with the Social Security Administration.

Insufficient Earnings and Profits (E&P)

Many tax schemes involve shareholders of closely held C corporations, where the corporation is used to deduct personal living expenses, and funds are distributed to the shareholders.

---

15. Treas. Reg. § 31.6051-2 (2019)

In *Boulware v. United States*, the Supreme Court held that corporate distributions could be taxable to the shareholder if certain rules apply.[16] The bottom line is that earnings and profits can be depleted without becoming taxable to the shareholder, but can be taxable after a certain amount is exceeded.

This is a technical issue that requires expert assistance, but special agents know that if a C corporation is making distributions to a shareholder, then calculations need to be completed to determine when and how much should be taxable to the shareholder. If the corporation lacked enough E&P, then the distributions are non-taxable to the defendant's benefit.

Key Takeaway: If the government is claiming that distributions were taxable to the defendant, the Boulware *case may be applicable.*

---

16. Boulware v. United States, 552 U.S. 421 (2008)

Chapter 14

Other Possible Pertinent Information

A s a non-lawyer, I add this section because it does involve information that exists, but may or may not be in discovery. Depending on who I ask, some attorneys would call it *Jencks* material, while other attorneys say it is privileged because it is part of the deliberation process. There are two major documents that are also maintained on the case agent's hard drive: the CCR Report and WLR. I will explain both.

CCR Report

Tax crimes have a long and thorough review process by various IRS-CI special agents, IRS legal counsel, and DOJ Tax Division. One of the reviewers is called CCR. CCR (Centralized Case Reviewer) is a special agent whose job is to review the investigative agent's prosecution report, opine on its merits, recommend changes, etc. It can be a treasure trove of good information about what weaknesses are in a case, because CCR is known to be unforgiving to the case agent. Agents don't enjoy CCR reviewing their cases for various reasons.

After reviewing the SAR, CCR prepares a report with their comments and suggestions, and sends the report back to the investigative agent and the supervisor. The agent is required to comment on CCR's report if the recommended changes were made and, if not, then why. IRM section 9.5.12.2 defines the review process.[1]

CCR's comments and the agent's replies are part of the case file that IRS-CI maintains electronically. CCRs are usually off-site, so documents to and from CCRs are kept in the special agent's and management's case file.

Key Takeaway: CCR may prove that your defense was a previous concern during the review process. Furthermore, it can also help you find potential defenses. If you cross-examine the investigative agent, his comments, actions or inactions may be disclosed. I would think it would be interesting if CCR was on the witness stand explaining their criticisms of the SAR.

Workload Review for Agent (WLR)

The IRS is a statistic driven agency. They may deny it, but statistics are used to promote their activity to Congress for future funding. And what gets measured, gets monitored. Good or bad, that is the way it works. IRS-CI is no different. IRS-CI special agents are limited in their time, so they only investigate a few cases a year. On average, it takes about 18 months to work a case from beginning to end. (The end being that the case is complete and is now ready for DOJ Tax Division's approval). IRS-CI management doesn't want a special agent to spend time on cases that have little prosecution potential. To combat bad cases and lazy agents, a quarterly case workload review (WLR) is conducted. This review is when the special agent meets with the supervisor to discuss the status of the investigation, such as weaknesses, analyzing bank records, obstacles, strengths, and strategy to increase prosecution potential.

---

1. Internal Revenue Service, U.S. Dep't of Treasury, Internal Revenue Manual § 9.5.12.2 (2019), available at https://www.irs.gov/irm/part9/irm_0 9-005-012.

Here are some questions that the supervisor will ask during the meeting:

- Are records available?

- Should this case be Grand Jury or Administrative?

- Have key witnesses (subject, co-conspirators, return preparers) been interviewed?

- Are search warrants needed?

- How is the analysis of records coming along?

- Are there *Greenberg* problems?

- What is the availability of witnesses during the investigation and at trial?

- If this case isn't moving as expected, then why the delay?

This is also a gold mine of information, like being in the office during candid discussions. The supervisor writes this information into CIMIS. CIMIS maintains the statistics, key points of the investigation, and actions recommended by supervisors. Supervisors and upper management have the ability to review cases at any time; that is why defense attorneys who think that they can sway IRS-CI management at the last minute usually will lose, because management is aware of the cases on a quarterly basis.

Agents write the various answers to the questions identified above. Management writes their thoughts, actions recommended, etc. into CIMIS. Agents don't have access to management's comments, being communications between the supervisor and the Special Agent in Charge (SAC) or Assistant (ASAC). If a case is late, has problems, etc. your access to the special agent's WLR or the supervisor's opinions would be beneficial. The supervisor writes a list of directives to the case agent to ensure that the case stays on track for completion.

Key takeaway: The agent and supervisor meet on a quarterly basis to discuss the merits of an investigation. The WLR documents will give you insight into the weaknesses, timeliness, etc. of an investigation. In my experience, the prosecution considers the agent's documents to be Jencks *material.*

So, you have reviewed all the evidence during the discovery process and the client is comfortable with your defense strategy. The next chapter covers the key aspects of a criminal tax trial.

Chapter 15

Trial

L et's assume that the defendant wants a trial on the criminal tax violations. Here are some issues that I personally have experienced or can foresee.

Reliance Defense

Reliance defense is when a taxpayer is limited in their knowledge of tax matters, and relies on someone else with better credentials and education for tax advice. Much like a car owner taking their vehicle to a mechanic because they lack the expertise to fix the car, the typical taxpayer is limited in their knowledge of tax matters so they hire a return preparer.

I personally sat in a courtroom gallery during a criminal trial where a defendant was moving money overseas and claiming deductions that were not legal. The defendant bought into a scheme sold by a charismatic "tax expert." The defense showed that the promoter of the scheme was a con artist, who previously pled guilty to assisting others in committing tax evasion and money laundering. The defense brought into the courtroom the defendant's return preparer, who was a CPA. The CPA testified that he believed that what the defendant was doing was legal. Furthermore, the defense brought another CPA who thought the same way. If the experts believed in its legality, how is a non-CPA supposed to know differently?

The defendant was later found not guilty. Although, it was obvious that the wealthy defendant was trying to evade taxes through other shady means, the jury believed that he had a reliance defense.

Return Preparers Have to Explain Mistakes

If a defendant signed a false tax return, the return preparer is the key witness who will explain how the tax return was prepared based on the documents received from the defendant. In my experience on complex tax investigations, CPAs who are the return preparers made mistakes on the tax returns. These mistakes can be immaterial, so the government admits those mistakes early in the trial before cross examination of the return preparer.

In small CPA firms, multiple people touch the books and records which are the basis of the preparation of the tax return. The defendant may be the direct contact or a representative may be the direct contact for various employees at the CPA firm. Typically, one or both contact the return preparer, but send the information to a secretary or staff accountant at the CPA firm. The information is then prepared by the staff accountant and reviewed by a senior member of the firm. Ultimately, the partner will sign the tax return. This chain of events can create problems if there is a dispute about what was given, what was told, and what was asked.

- What documents were given?

- What was told to anyone in the firm?

- Was key information in email or was it verbal?

- Did the return preparer ask the pertinent questions during their due diligence?

These types of questions should be answered in the special agent's prosecution report, and for sure should be addressed at trial.

This is particularly troublesome if the questionable amount on the tax return has no documentary basis. For example, gross receipts are reported for $1 million on the tax return but the return preparer had no documented evidence for that sales amount, but does have documented evidence for other numbers.

Return Preparer Problems

From the initial allegation to a trial, investigations can take years to complete. Some witnesses die or have memory problems. I had a few cases where the return preparers were older, which caused me concern about the physical and mental health problems that come with age.

The IRS does not require a competency test to become a return preparer. Anyone can call themselves a return preparer. Usually IRS-CI discontinues cases that have incompetent return preparers. The return preparer may not have the expertise on the tax subject matter. Furthermore, they may not be current in the tax law. I have interviewed return preparers who didn't have a college degree, had no formal tax training, and only started preparing tax returns a few weeks earlier. The level of expertise runs the gamut.

One time, I interviewed a return preparer who rounded expenses up to the nearest 1,000. Therefore, all the business deductions were nice even round numbers. When asked why, she stated that she was trained that way by another return preparer. I could only shake my head in disbelief.

Verbage Confusion

Before I became a special agent, I was a CPA and also taught accounting to college students. What I discovered in teaching was that words mean different things depending on the context and what type of accounting was discussed. Even the same words within the IRS can have different meanings. A SAR can be a suspicious activity report or a special agent's report.

Accounting has various sub-disciplines: cost accounting, tax accounting, financial accounting, and forensic accounting. Each sub-discipline has their unique language and lexicon.

For example, the word "cost" is defined differently depending on who you ask. For financial accounting it can be the cost of an item which includes shipping costs, setup costs, and possibly interest. In tax accounting, cost is often confused with basis, which could be the same or different than cost. When a person inherits an asset, the cost is zero to the recipient, but the basis is equal to the fair market value at time of death.

Let's take the phrase "gross income" as an example. According to tax law, gross income means all income from all types of sources, unless excluded by statute. However, not all gross income becomes taxable income. On a credit application, gross income is considered to be gross wages. But can "gross income" on a credit application be confused with gross income in tax language? Put another way, a self-employed person may have sales of $1 million and a net income of $200,000. The $1 million amount is considered gross income for taxes, but on a credit application, the proper context is more likely the $200,000 net income. The applicant may have placed $1 million believing that is the true number. I have never experienced this argument by either the prosecution or defense, but during trials when it could be relevant, I have always wondered if the defense would make that argument and how the government could best make a rebuttal.

In essence, the business language that is used can be defined differently than by the general public.

Cash on Hand

What a defendant owns in cash before an investigation is key to a cash hoard defense, when cash purchases or cash deposits are used in a criminal tax trial. If there are large amounts of cash that need to be investigated, a special agent will try to get the cash on hand amount nailed down from the defendant during an initial interview or using financial records to show that cash on hand was either nonexistent or, at least, the same throughout the investigative period. When using various indirect methods of proof, cash on hand becomes relevant.

In forensic accounting, there are different methods of proof. The US Supreme Court has allowed various methods of proof to show unreported income. The most common method of proof is specific item. This is when the prosecution can show a direct correlation between the income or deduction based on direct evidence. However, there are times when there are no books and records, and the defendant has a cash lifestyle. In those cases, cash deposits or cash payments are calculated using indirect methods of proof. Three main indirect methods are: net worth method of proof, bank deposit method of proof, and expenditures method of proof.

IRM section 9.5.9 shows the different methods of proof. What is interesting is that cash deposits are very important in the net worth method of proof, bank deposit method of proof, and expenditures method of proof.[1] If the prosecution is using cash as part of its tax calculation, then you should hire an expert to review the government's assumptions and analysis.

A cash hoard defense and how it affects the criminal tax loss is too complicated to explain fully in this book. Just know that if the government is using an indirect method of proof to calculate unreported income, then cash on hand becomes important. The larger the amount of cash on hand is at the beginning, the more difficult it is for the prosecution.

In a cash hoard defense, the age of the currency found during a search warrant can be an indicator of whether the defense is legitimate. If a defendant claims that they have been saving the cash since their teenage years, the print date on the cash would be consistent with older currency. A reasonable person would expect cash saved for 20 years to have print dates of currency over 20 years old.

---

1. Internal Revenue Service, U.S. Dep't of Treasury, Internal Revenue Manual § 9.5.9 (2020), available at https://www.irs.gov/irm/part9/irm_09-0 05-009

Cash Disbursements

Because of *Greenberg*, cash disbursements are typically considered to be business deductions. The prosecution has the burden of proof beyond a reasonable doubt that the cash withdrawn from bank accounts was used for personal living expenses. To be successful, IRS-CI will have to show a correlation between the cash withdrawals and cash purchases of large items, such as vehicles, jewelry, etc.

Early in my career in IRS-CI, I had an investigation where a defendant was in the construction business. The business income was from large checks, which were deposited into the business bank accounts. However, the defendant would write checks to cash, which the government suspected was used for personal living expenses. I interviewed his employees and all the known sub-contractors. None of them admitted being paid in cash. He also had an agreement with his employees where he received 50% of the net profit and the employees would receive the other half in salary. My investigation showed that the defendant's cash lifestyle was spent on women and alcohol, but not much else was known about where the cash went. He blew through it. He was on the government's radar because the case also involved fraud. I was brought in to assist in the grand jury investigation because the defendant also failed to file personal and business tax returns. The defendant was insulated from the day-to-day operations that caused the fraud. There were no formal books and records because they were destroyed. I had to recreate them using only bank records. After totaling all the cash withdrawals (which equaled his employees' salaries) and proving that he never paid his sub-contractors and employees in cash, the prosecution was comfortable with the idea that all the cash disbursements to him were indeed for his personal living expenses and subject to the criminal tax computation. This approach was rare, but it was approved.

In today's growing cashless society, cash disbursements are becoming less and less relevant because society is steering away from cash and is now using debit and credit cards for purchases.

Cash Deposits

As stated before, a cash hoard is a defense to criminal tax investigations if the prosecution is assuming that cash deposits or cash purchases are taxable income. Proving cash deposits are taxable income can be difficult when large cash withdrawals exist. I had a case where a medical professional was depositing large amounts of cash and withdrawing large amounts of cash. Sole proprietors in the medical profession receive income from copays and insurance payments. The volume of cash for this type of business was unusual. During my initial interview of the taxpayer, he stated that he was going through a divorce from his second wife and was hiding funds from her. He would withdraw large amounts of cash, keep it in his closet, and sometimes would redeposit the cash if he needed to pay bills on time. The taxpayer reported substantial amount of income every year, so I closed the case. The cash deposits were not from sales, but instead from his cash withdrawals being redeposited.

Introduction of Documents

The introduction of documents into evidence can be tricky. Without going into detail, if the defense needs to introduce document evidence, be sure to be on firm footing to get it introduced. In one case, I had a signature card on a bank account that was unsigned. It caused problems trying to prove the defendant's control of the account: even though the defendant's name was on the card, the lack of signature was enough to cast doubt on the defendant's control..

In my experience, IRS-CI does a great job knowing what evidence needs to be introduced and who is going to introduce it. What makes them successful is their understanding of how to introduce evidence to prove the elements of the tax violations. Their prosecution reports are focused on what the witness will testify to and what documents will be introduced by that witness. On the other hand, I have seen criminal defense attorneys (particularly those who practice mostly in state court) struggle trying to introduce certain documents into evidence because the document either wasn't the right one or the witness would be the wrong person to introduce it. This may be obvious to many criminal defense attorneys, but federal court is very particular about how evidence is introduced and who introduces it.

Books and Records

In most tax investigations, books and records exist in some type of digital format. The most common bookkeeping software for small businesses is QuickBooks. Sometimes, the special agent has to recreate the books and records because those records don't exist or are not available. If books and records already exist, some books and records may have multiple people with access to them and the capability to change or edit them. If multiple people had access to the records, the accuracy and responsibility have to be considered, particularly if both spouses use the same software. If a potential key witness is the spouse of the defendant, IRS-CI and the AUSA are cautious of these arrangements.

As a special agent, it was always a problem when multiple parties (especially family members) were involved in the creation of the books and records, how those books and records were given to the return preparer, and how the return preparer used those books and records to file tax returns.

Search Warrant Results Tainted?

I previously discussed the typical process from the beginning of the search warrant to the analysis of those seized records. The weak link in the evidence gathered during the search warrant is the chain of custody and lack of documentation when evidence is reviewed and stored. In the previous chapter on discovery, I go into more detail about the concerns.

Getting Witnesses Present (RPP Investigations)

In return preparer investigations, the typical witness/victim is from a poor neighborhood, possibly has a criminal history, has personal problems that need professional help, lacks consistent employment, and may be on government assistance. For the government, getting these witnesses to show up on time in court, dressed appropriately, and in a right frame of mind, can be challenging. This does not include finding them in the first place to serve a trial subpoena and prepare them as a witness. During trial with these types of cases, it is not uncommon for IRS-CI to play a glorified taxi service. Special agents will travel to pick up and drop off witnesses to ensure the witnesses are present in court. With any investigation, the government will create a list of witnesses that they will expect to call to testify, then the witness list is pared down even more because getting these witness to court with credible testimony is challenging.

RPP Witnesses got Same Deal Somewhere Else

The crux of the government's case in return preparer investigations is that the return preparer was the catalyst in preparing a false tax return. The witness in the trial is portrayed as a victim of a bad return preparer, who also victimizes the IRS by causing the issuance of a false refund. The prosecution's narrative is: if it wasn't for the bad return preparer, the witness would have been happy with a true and accurate refund or would have happily paid the tax due if required. In these cases, there is a willful blindness by the witness to the large refund. If it is too good to be true, it probably is, but something for nothing is very enticing to people. That being said, as part of a return preparer trial the credibility of the witnesses is key to the conviction of the defendant.

In one of my investigations in the pre-trial stage, the prosecution attorney requested that I analyze all tax returns of the witnesses at least one year prior to the alleged criminal violation. He wanted to determine if these witnesses were possibly getting the same scheme somewhere else. He wanted to head off any potential defenses that the witness was participating in the fraud by expecting fraud to be committed. As a special agent, I gathered that information, which didn't result in any impeaching evidence, but nevertheless it was a good tactic to cover his bases before putting the witness on the stand. From that experience, I recommended this technique to other new prosecutors that had similar cases.

If all your work results in a guilty plea or the defendant is found guilty, then some of the same information that you have reviewed will also be relevant for sentencing, which is the next chapter.

Chapter 16

Sentencing

So, the client has pled guilty or was found guilty, and the sentencing phase is now starting. What are the key things that should be reviewed during this process?

Some steps in this chapter have already been addressed in more detail in previous chapters. If that is the case, a brief explanation will be given, and you will be referred to previous chapters. Let's look at some key areas during the sentencing process.

MFTRA -C

Get an updated MFTRA -C. The importance of a MFTRA -C has already been discussed in this book. Hopefully, the special agent will be agreeable to pull that information for you. If a MFTRA -C is not available, then request a regular transcript, which can be requested from the special agent or can be accessed from the IRS web portal if the proper POA is filed. You are looking for any substantive actions on the transcript, such as payments being posted, tax returns posted, etc. The transcript can verify if anything has happened (which it shouldn't have) since the investigation started. Remember, when IRS-CI opens a subject criminal investigation, a 914 control code is placed on the defendant's account to stop civil activity. Getting a transcript is ensuring that you are aware of all activity since the discovery stage.

Payments Made

Tax loss and restitution are important at the sentencing phase. What is the true loss or attempted loss to the government or other victims? Out of the tax loss, how much is still owed for restitution purposes?

When sentencing starts, substantial time has passed and the IRS-CI special agent has focused on other cases. When the case is picked up again for the sentencing phase, tax payments may have occurred between the date of the crime and the sentencing date. To me, this is a very time-consuming process because it requires manual calculations from the tax transcripts. Before sentencing, the IRS-CI special agent should update their spreadsheet of tax payments for the following reasons:

Payments reduce any potential restitution and possible loss. Whenever the IRS civil side applies tax payments, they are applied to the penalties and interest first, then to the principal. On many occasions, the prosecuting attorney will ask the case agent to apply any payments to the principal first so that a conservative calculation is made for the judge. Also, payments associated with employment taxes are applied by the civil side to the employer taxes first, then to the trust fund taxes. A defense attorney should want the defendant's payments to be applied to the trust fund amount first. This can greatly reduce the tax loss and restitution calculation for unpaid payroll taxes.

By the time of sentencing, witnesses may have paid tax liabilities in RPP investigations. The time between the tax crime and sentencing could be years. In the meantime, the IRS could have collected taxes from the victims whose false tax return had been filed for a fraudulent refund. The IRS would continue to collect any tax deficiencies from the witness, not knowing that there is an underlying criminal tax investigation on the return preparer. The defendant's tax transcripts are frozen with the 914 control codes. However, in RPP investigations, the freeze is not on the witness's account. Therefore, the IRS would garnish wages, keep subsequent tax refunds to apply to the tax liabilities, etc. Such payments should be taken into consideration at sentencing because the government has been paid, either partially or in full, from the victims by the time of sentencing.

Evasion of Payment

The sentencing guidelines for tax evasion (evasion of payment) are based on the total tax due at the time of the evasion. However, I learned from a good defense attorney that a lesser amount is possible. I had a case where the defendant pled guilty to tax evasion. The scheme was selling real estate that was subject to a federal tax lien, but the true sales price of the property was greater than the sales contract. The defendant was to receive additional proceeds at closing "under the table." The defendant owed the IRS approximately $1 million, but successfully received $350,000 "under the table" after closing. The prosecution argued that the sentencing should be for $1 million. The defense attorney successfully persuaded the judge that the defendant should be sentenced based on the amount taken ($350,000) and not the full amount of tax owed ($1,000,000).

Compare PSR to SAR

This one I learned the hard way. Fortunately, any errors discovered after sentencing were always in favor of the defendant, which didn't require the US Attorney's Office to petition the judge to amend the restitution.

When a defendant pleads guilty or is found guilty, the US Attorney's Office sends information to the US Probation Office (USPO) for a pre-sentence report (PSR). In theory, the USPO receives the relevant information to prepare an accurate report. However, many times this is not the case for the following reasons:

The USPO doesn't enjoy preparing PSR for tax crimes. It is a very different animal than guns and drugs because it can be complicated determining tax loss (sometimes estimated) and restitution. Tax crime PSRs require an understanding of accounting, taxes, and business law, and are prone to errors if the probation officer has no formal education in these areas. I have never met a USPO officer that enjoyed creating a PSR for tax crimes.

The US Attorney's Office sends a document dump to the USPO, which may or may not be accurate or timely. Sometimes the document dump, which can easily exceed 1,000 pages, is incompatible with the computer system, for example, because of encryption, which causes miscommunication and frustration between the USAO, USPO, and IRS-CI. The volume of documents to review is very frustrating for those who don't review white collar crimes often.

The PSR is sealed and is not available to the investigative agent. Unless the AUSA reveals the relevant section for tax loss, the agent will never see it. Therefore, if the AUSA does not get clarification from the investigative agent about the correct numbers, how they were calculated, etc., then the PSR could be subject to various errors.

A best practice is to read the SAR and compare it to the PSR. Also ask for updated tax loss and restitution amounts (broken down by year and type of tax) to ensure that the PSR is correct.

6020B vs Reality

U.S.C. Title 26, section 6020(b) has been discussed already in this book. In summary, using a 6020B calculation as the basis for a tax loss will most likely result in an overstated tax loss. If your case involves a 6020B calculation by the civil side of the IRS, get an expert to recalculate that loss for a more reasonable amount.

Can the Loss be Tied to the Defendant?

At sentencing, the standard for tying the loss amount to the defendant is what was "reasonably foreseeable." It can be very difficult for a defendant to argue that they did not know the loss would be as much or as bad as it was. I saw this argument made quite often in cases involving conspiracies among return preparers.

A tax preparation business establishes itself in a neighborhood and starts hiring employees. Because of the turnover and seasonal nature of the business, employees come and go, and some employees may or may not work the whole tax season, which is January through April. To grow the business rapidly, the tax preparation shop needs customers who are promised large tax refunds. Customers getting large tax refunds share their success story with others, which leads to more customers coming to the return preparation shop. Once the fraudulent behavior is learned, the scheme spreads to other return preparers.

Herein lies the problem: Return Preparer A prepares a few tax returns that are false, and Return Preparer B prepares many more. If the defense can argue that A is a lesser offender, there can be a reduction of A's sentence. Furthermore, tax returns that are filed with the IRS are required to have a "Paid Return Preparer" signature on the form. Many times, the Return Preparer section is false because if B files a false tax return, B will most likely use A's name. So, it looks like A was preparing most of the tax returns, when in fact it was B.

This gets kind of tricky, but in my opinion, laying out the facts that A is a victim of most of the false tax returns attributed to A by the government goes a long way, especially on the front end, during plea negotiations. The bottom line is: don't take it at face value that the government's estimate of total tax loss based on the "paid return preparer" section is accurate. In these types of schemes, it is probably not. The best way to negate false attribution is to interview witnesses to determine if they can identify A or B as the return preparer. It should also be in the investigating agent's memos that this scheme was happening. Many times the witnesses cannot positively identify either A or B as the return preparer, especially if A and B are in the same age range and are the same race and gender.

Sometimes there is controversy regarding the link in the chain between how information is received and placed on the tax return. For example: who delivered the documents to the return preparer? Did someone else receive the documents first at the return preparers office, like a receptionist? Where is the supporting documentation? Were there any conversations during the initial meeting or any thereafter that could have changed the numbers? Did a manager review the tax returns and change the numbers after the initial return preparer submitted for final review before processing it with the IRS? All of these possible problems are common in return preparer schemes.

Extrapolation Problems

In return preparer investigations, there may be hundreds or thousands of false returns that were filed on an annual basis before the defendant was caught. IRS-CI cannot possibly audit or verify these tax returns to find an accurate tax loss. Because the courts have allowed extrapolation to estimate the tax loss,[1] IRS-CI has established procedures for a statistical analysis to calculate the tax loss for sentencing purposes. The rules for this analysis are not available in a public document.

Special agents are not statisticians, but IRS does have statisticians on their payroll. To ensure their analysis is accurate, IRS-CI will request guidance from one of their statisticians on how to conduct a sample and extrapolate those findings to calculate an estimated tax loss.

As a practical matter, the extrapolation is a headache for special agents. I have learned that if the scheme is from false education credits, then instead of conducting a statistical sample, I would calculate the difference between what the IRS received from the educational institution and what was reported on the tax return. But each return preparation scheme is different. If the special agent has calculated a tax loss at sentencing, ask if the tax loss was from an extrapolation and the basis for those calculations.

Reasonable Calculation

Tax loss drives the sentencing guidelines. The sentencing guidelines state that if the tax loss needs to be estimated, a percentage of the unreported income or

---

1. United States v. Bryant, 128 F.3d 74, 75-76 (2d Cir. 1997)

deductions can be used for that purpose; this is mentioned in section 2T1.1 of the federal sentencing guidelines.[2]

Relevant Conduct

Relevant conduct can include the tax loss outside the statute of limitations. It can also include unpaid state taxes,[3] self-employment taxes,[4] and delinquent social security taxes.[5]

Taxpayer on Hook Civilly

Once the J&C (Judgment and Commitment order) has been entered for Title 26 violations, IRS-CI will wait until the sentencing appeal deadline has expired. Once it has expired, the case agent will close the case and forward the J&C, factual basis, and plea agreement to the civil side. IRS-CI will also release its control over the account, and request that the civil side archive its files related to the defendant because of the criminal judgment. The J&C should explicitly detail the type of tax, amount, and tax period, which is used to assess the tax on the defendant's transcripts. Most of the time, the J&C has a total amount. However, if the J&C does not detail the type of tax, amount, etc., at least, the special agent should have a spreadsheet that lists those details. A code 910 is placed on the taxpayer's account, which tells the IRS to keep all master files on the investigation.

---

2. U. S. Sentencing Comm'n, Guidelines Manual § 2T1.1 (2021)

3. United States v. Fuentes, 107 F.3d 1515, 1526 (11th Cir. 1997) (state offenses that are part of the same course of conduct as federal offenses and part of a common scheme or plan must be considered relevant conduct)

4. United States v. Twieg, 238 F.3d 930 (7th Cir. 2001)

5. United States v. Martin-Rios, 143 F.2d 662 (2d Cir. 1998)

When civil receives the closing documents, it is free to pursue civil collection activity. Under *Klein v. Commissioner*, penalties and interest cannot be automatic on the restitution amount.[6] In other words, *Klein* disallowed the civil side piling on. However, the civil side can use its collection powers to file liens, garnish wages, levy bank accounts, etc., once IRS-CI closes its case.

I believe that most defendants are not aware of what happens once the J&C is ordered. IRM section 4.8.6.1.2 states the authority to assess a criminal tax restitution on certain tax crimes.[7] For most tax crimes, the IRS has the authority to assess the judgment as a tax.[8] Once the J&C is issued with the IRS listed as the victim, the civil side is unleashed to collect taxes. I say this, because if the client has substantial means to pay the taxes, the client can expect the restitution amount from the J&C to be a green light for the civil side to collect. This is why it is very important that the J&C be a reasonable amount, particularly if the client has substantial wealth. I have noticed that prosecutors and special agents are not firm on the restitution amount because the hard work is over (getting a guilty verdict). Any attempt to collect payment on those unpaid taxes is another person's problem, not theirs.

The J&C for restitution has a 20-year civil statute of limitations from the date of the J&C entered by the court.[9] This gives the Department of Justice the opportunity to collect using their Financial Litigation Unit to find assets and income.

After sentencing, the defendant's case is not entirely forgotten by IRS-CI. The case agent will continue to have the investigation listed on his inventory, possibly for years, to monitor the conditions of probation. If payments are

---

6. Klein v. Commissioner, 149 T.C. No. 15 (2017)

7. Internal Revenue Service, U.S. Dep't of Treasury, Internal Revenue Manual § 4.8.6.1.2 (2020), available at https://www.irs.gov/irm/part4/irm_0 4-008-006.

8. I.R.C. § 6201(a)(4) (2022)

9. 18 U.S.C. § 3613(b) (2022)

required by the court, IRS-CI will monitor those payments to ensure that the defendant is in tax compliance. If payments are not made per the J&C, then IRS-CI will verify the non-payment and notify the US Attorney's Office that the defendant is not complying with the court order. The US Attorney's Office can then pursue the violation of the court order. Once the probation period has elapsed, IRS-CI will stop monitoring the defendant's conditions of supervised release.

As a side note, if the tax investigation involved an RPP investigation, where the defendant was a return preparer, then the restitution assessment and any subsequent payments would be recorded on the witness/victim's transcripts. This means that if the witness/victim makes a payment to their tax account, the defendant will not be required to pay that amount as well.

Chapter 17

Summary

A s a defense attorney, you have options to help your client throughout the criminal tax investigation. The primary focus should be to get them into tax compliance early before a criminal tax referral is made. This can be completed by filing the missing tax returns, amending the tax returns, and engaging in a tax payment plan.

If your client is a subject in a criminal tax investigation, look for reasonable excuses to persuade IRS-CI or the AUSA to close the investigation. Such excuses could include health reasons, inability to establish responsibility, low tax loss, or a reliance on a return preparer. But if the government believes in its investigation, expect over 18 months for it to be ready for indictment. In the meantime, keep a pleasant, open dialog throughout the process.

If you assist your client during discovery, review the current evidence, such as the special agent's report, to evaluate the viability of the investigation. If necessary, ask for more information that may not be in the discovery files. Then, proceed as necessary based on your knowledge of all the facts.

Before sentencing, review the tax loss, restitution calculations, and the defendant's role in the scheme.

Throughout the investigation and court process, hiring an expert to advise you in representing your client will be well worth the cost. An expert under a *Kovel* agreement can help craft a reasonable argument or tax calculation to give your client their best chance at a fair outcome.

With all this knowledge, no matter what stage of the investigation that the defendant is in, you should have a good basis for advising your client and crafting reasonable responses to the AUSA and the courts for a fair resolution.

If you are in need for expert assistance in criminal tax or forensic accounting matters, you can go to www.nordlandercpa.com or www.robertnordlander.com for more details.

Request

Before you go...

If you have received benefit from this book, please recommend this book to a friend and leave a review on Amazon or your favorite bookstore's website. Within two minutes, there is an easy way to leave a review through www.ro bertnordlander.com/review.

Word of mouth and referrals are the lifeblood of the forensic accounting industry. Your thoughts and recommendations are always appreciated.

For your continuing education, you can also listen to the *Fraud Fighter Podcast* (which focuses on the forensic accounting industry) and the *Criminal Tax Files* podcast (which all about criminal tax matters). Both podcasts are on every major podcast directory, such as Apple, Spotify, and Google. It will be a pleasure of have you as a listener. As part of the criminal tax community, your recommendation on topics and potential guests is always welcomed.

More details about the author and podcasts can be found at:

- www.nordlandercpa.com

- www.fraudfighterpodcast.com

- www.robertnordlander.com

Discovery Checklist

The following checklist can assist you in your discovery process. This checklist is directly related to this book's chapter on discovery. A similar checklist is also available online at www.nordlandercpa.com/discovery.

Checklist

1. Special Agent's Prosecution Report

2. Special Agent's Diary

3. Emails and Texts

4. Bank Account Reconciliations

5. Tax Return Reconciliations

6. Employment Tax 6020B Calculations (if applicable)

7. Check for *Greenberg* Problems

8. Review IRS Civil Tax File and *Tweel* Problems (if applicable)

9. Search Warrant Results (paper documents at agent's office)

10. Search Warrant Results (from electronic devices)

11. Search Warrant Evidence Chain of Custody

12. Undercover Operations (audio and video recording)

13. Special Agents' Handwritten Notes (at agent's office)

14. Spouse's Filed Tax Returns

15. Verify Statute of Limitations

16. Earnings and Profits calculation (*Boulware* decision, if applicable)

Other Possible Pertinent Information

1. CCR's Report and Special Agent's Response

2. Workload Review

About the Author

Robert Nordlander spent over 20 years as a special agent with IRS-Criminal Investigation. He investigated various tax crimes ranging from simple embezzlement to tax evasion using foreign trusts. He is an author, speaker, podcast host, and consultant to attorneys who need forensic accounting and criminal tax expertise. He has a CPA license, CFE certification, and MBA degree. He is the principal member of Nordlander CPA, PLLC, a boutique forensic accounting and tax resolution practice.

Robert Nordlander earned a Bachelor of Science degree in Accounting at Bob Jones University. Afterwards, he was part of a small CPA firm, where he prepared tax returns, conducted audits, and represented his clients with the IRS. It was during that time, he earned his CPA license and an MBA degree from the University of North Carolina at Greensboro. He later applied to be a special agent with IRS-Criminal Investigation. During the two year hiring process, he went back to Bob Jones University to teach various accounting and tax courses.

After six months of training at the Federal Law Enforcement Center, his first post of duty was in Birmingham, Alabama, where he investigated tax evasion, identity theft, and false tax returns. Shortly after 9/11, he was temporarily assigned to the FBI Joint Terrorism Task Force to investigate possible terrorism financing. He later transferred to Greensboro, North Carolina, where he finished the rest of his special agent career.

During his IRS-CI career, he was given various assignments, such as working with the Cyber Crime Unit in Washington, DC, Cyber Crime Coordinator of the Charlotte Field Office, Use of Force Coordinator, and lead investigator on a bank SAR-Review Team. Using his teaching background, Nordlander also developed and taught courses for IRS-CI for continuing education. He was also tasked to teach anti-money laundering and tax courses overseas in conjunction with the Department of State and IRS-Criminal Investigation. He was the recipient of various awards from IRS-CI, the State of North Carolina, and US Attorney's Offices.

In the later stages of his successful special agent career, he started the *Fraud Fighter Podcast*, which focuses on the forensic accounting industry. Shortly after retirement, he continued the podcast and started Nordlander CPA, PLLC. Following some of his podcast guests' advice, he earned the CFE credential.

He continues to teach forensic accounting and tax resolution subjects. Attorney and CPA associations frequently request his presentations on cryptocurrency and criminal tax matters. He recently started a second podcast: *Criminal Tax Files*. This podcast discusses federal criminal tax matters.

To keep a life balance, he finished (albeit slow) various long distance races: a marathon, multiple half-marathons, and triathlons. He is married and has one daughter. He is a fan of great BBQ, the FIRE movement, and anything about J.R.R. Tolkien and C.S. Lewis.

If you have a need for a speaker or expertise in forensic accounting and criminal tax matters, he can be reached at www.nordlandercpa.com or www.robertnordlander.com.

Made in United States
North Haven, CT
20 June 2025

69999938R00085